Diving Guide
to the
Eastern Caribbean

Martha Watkins Gilkes

CARIBBEAN

First published 1994

Published by THE MACMILLAN PRESS LTD
London and Basingstoke
*Associated companies and representatives in Accra,
Auckland, Delhi, Dublin, Gaborone, Hamburg, Harare,
Hong Kong, Kuala Lumpur, Lagos, Manzini, Melbourne,
Mexico City, Nairobi, New York, Singapore, Tokyo.*

ISBN 0–333–55467–1

Printed in Hong Kong

A catalogue record for this book is available
from the British Library

Acknowledgements

The author and publishers wish to acknowledge, with thanks, the
following photographic sources:
Alice Bagshaw, George Hume, Tony Gilkes, John Shears, Lucy Byng.
All unattributed photographs are by Martha Watkins Gilkes.

Front cover photograph by Alice Bagshaw.
Back cover photograph of Martha Watkins Gilkes and Stan Waterman by
Yorie Pigott.
Back cover photograph of Martha Watkins Gilkes with Peter Benchley and
Teddy Tucker by John Shears.

Contents

Stan Waterman and Martha Watkins Gilkes
(YORIE PIGOTT)

I dedicate this book to Stan Waterman my diving buddy, long-time friend and mentor in diving.

Over the past 14 years of our diving-oriented friendship, he has introduced me to a myriad of marine creatures from docile invertebrate life to fierce man-eating sharks! We have shared moments of terror and moments of magic in our exploration of the underwater world. My quest for more will never cease, thanks to his inspiration.

Acknowledgements

The production of this diving guide would have been inconceivable without the help, guidance, knowledge and hours of assistance of the many people involved with it. I wish to express my sincere gratitude to them all.

While I have personally visited and dived every island written about, it would not have been possible to visit every single location described in this guide. I have relied on the guidance of established and reputable dive operators, instructors and dive masters to describe their favourite locations on the various islands. To all the dive shops which played an important part in providing this information, I express my gratitude. I am especially grateful to Bill Tewes of Dive St Vincent and to Bob Gascoine, owner of Aquanaut in the Turks and Caicos Islands.

I would also like to thank all the photographers who have given permission for their outstanding work to be included in this book.

Sincere thanks go to Edna Fortescue, Publisher of *F.T. Caribbean*, who inspired the project years ago and encouraged me to pursue it, to Tony Syrett and Marney Macy for their invaluable computer assistance and to Marney in particular for the many hours of proofreading and 'helpful criticism', which was greatly appreciated. I could not leave out my husband Tony who not only put up with my various moods during the writing of this book, but also encouraged me on my endless travels. Many thanks to the very many, too numerous to name individually, who helped make this happen.

In writing this guide, I wish to open up more of the exciting underwater world to the diving fraternity, by giving information about some places which have hardly ever been written about. Enjoy safe diving!

Foreword

Strange as it seems the Caribbean, perhaps the most popular diving area in the world for the greatest number of divers, has had no guide, island by island, to its splendid dive locations. There have been several fish identification books but an objective, non-commercial description of the islands' dive spots and facilities has been strangely lacking. Until now, no one with wide-ranging knowledge of the islands and the creative energy to produce such a guide has come forth. Martha Watkins Gilkes has done just that in *Diving Guide to the Eastern Caribbean*. Her work as a consultant with the US State Department over a period of more than 20 years provided an intimate acquaintance with most of the islands. Stationed in Barbados she ranged throughout the Caribbean on diplomatic and policy missions. During those years she fell wildly in love with the underwater marine world and honed her skill as a diver and an underwater photographer. We have both dived and worked with Martha on many productions and watched with pleasure her superb grace in the sea and her unremitting sense of responsibility as a dive buddy. She is the penultimate dive companion. It came as no surprise to us that she ultimately became the driving force behind the establishment of the first diver recompression chamber on Barbados and the formation of the Caribbean Safe Diving Association.

Her dedication to diving introduced her to the dive masters of those islands and in turn to exploring the finest of the dive sites. The book is a treasure trove of accurate information from hands-on experience by one of the most respected divers in the Caribbean. Further, it is a loving tribute to the beautiful, vibrant marine environment of the Caribbean and the lush green islands that sit like jewels in the turquoise sea.

Stan Waterman

Peter Benchley

Introduction to Scuba Diving

This guide is intended to open up the world of scuba diving to many remote places where diving is just beginning to develop. In some cases, small dive shops have been established for a long time – some for as long as 15 years – and have operated on a very small scale, as many of the islands are only now becoming known as diving destinations.

There is limited information on the diving available on many of the islands which are cited in this book, and certainly, at the time of going to press, no other guide gives as much information on the most popular reef and wreck diving sites, or covers as many undeveloped islands in such great detail.

This guide is unique in several aspects. All too often, information on diving destinations is given by writers who are outsiders to the island and who after a whirlwind tour, write with limited knowledge. In addition, while most are certified divers, few are instructors and can approach diving from the safety aspect.

In the case of the present author, Martha Watkins Gilkes is an authority on the islands, having lived on four of them – Grenada, Barbados, St Lucia and presently Antigua – in the Eastern Caribbean region for the past 20 years. She has personally, and in most cases extensively, dived every island mentioned in this book. She is a certified PADI instructor and has owned and operated her own scuba business since 1979 on two islands (Barbados and Antigua). As President of the ECSDA (the Eastern Caribbean Safe Diving Association) since its inception in 1984, she has been involved with all aspects of diving safety on these islands.

The ECSDA was indeed instrumental in establishing a recompression chamber located in Barbados, which is used by many of the islands. It has also set up a recommended list of minimum safe standards for diving operators in Barbados, with the hope of expanding this regionally.

This in-depth personal knowledge of the Caribbean region, scuba diving and safety awareness in the sport makes this guide unique.

Scuba diving is fast becoming the 'in' sport with the numbers of divers dramatically increasing in recent years. While still male dominated, it has also attracted an increasingly larger number of women. Diving equipment is now produced with the female diver in mind; it is becoming less bulky, smaller, easier to handle and even fashionable with colour co-ordination. Health considerations for women are similar to those for the male diver, although diving while pregnant is not recommended as limited research has been done on the effects.

The epitome of a scuba dive is in clear, tropical waters on a colourful reef abounding with life. The Caribbean is a scuba diver's paradise, for there is a conglomeration of islands, surrounded by living reefs and providing different types of diving to suit everyone's dreams. In addition most of the islands cited in this book have not yet turned into 'diving circuses' as has happened in some of the more developed northern Caribbean islands, where 30 to 40 divers are herded onto large boats and dropped on 'package diving sites' where 'tame fish come for a hand-out of cheese squeeze'. Rather, most of the islands mentioned here are still virginal, in a diving sense, which makes for an exciting undersea adventure.

This, on the other hand, can also lead to frustration as the more remote islands lack any facilities, thus making the diving more difficult and basic. Sometimes equipment is not properly maintained and the majority of the islands, mentioned in this guide, have no regulations or guidance for the diving industry. This can lead to 'cowboy-type' operators running without qualified instructors and properly maintained and tested equipment. However, these destinations often offer the best diving. It is important to check on the level of competence of an operator and on the training of the 'instructor'. It is, indeed, a good idea, to request to see the certificates of the training instructor if these are not displayed. Some dive shops are associated with the major training organizations (PADI 5 star Facility or NAUI Dream Shop), which are guarantees of a certain standard of professionalism. Although the operators listed at the end of each chapter are legitimate and safety-oriented, it must be noted that this can change overnight.

Good health is a must for diving, but it is a myth that one needs to be a super-man or woman. It is however important to have healthy lungs and sinus and to be able to equalize one's ears, by gently blowing air into the eustachian tubes while blocking the nose. A medical examination by a physician trained in hyperbaric (diving) medicine is recommended and required by many instructors before taking up the sport. Scuba divers should always refrain from drinking alcoholic beverages before diving and it is preferable to limit alcoholic intake immediately after a dive, as this can bring on decompression sickness, if the diver is 'on the edge' with the level of nitrogen absorption. Care must also be taken when taking prescription drugs and medical advice should be sought.

It is a good idea to be trained in basic first-aid and CPR (Cardiac Pulmonary Resuscitation) as diving often takes place in remote locations where medical help is not easily obtained. First-aid equipment should always be part of standard gear. Most diving-related accidents are minor – scrapes and cuts on coral – but one should be prepared for dealing with these as well as more serious ones such as stings and bites from marine life, which can sometimes be life-threatening.

A good basic swimming ability is necessary, although one does not need to be an olympic swimmer!

Most scuba diving organizations offer several types of courses. A 'Resort Course' or 'Discover Scuba Experience' provides basic instruction in a short, condensed version (about 3 hours); it comprises a minimum of academic knowledge, a confined-water session (usually in a swimming pool) and an open water scuba dive. For more advanced diving, such as night dive, deep dive, or wreck dive, full certification and training in these various speciality areas are necessary.

Many tourists take the 'Resort Course' or 'Discover Scuba' as they have not got time to do a full certification course, which requires written exams, classroom lectures, several confined-water sessions and a number of scuba dives. If one is seriously interested, a full certification course should be taken.

The major training agencies recommend that children should be at least 12 years old to dive. An upper-age limit is, however, no longer a serious consideration, assuming one is in good health, able to deal with the equipment and to get on and off boats. Even physical handicaps are not a limiting factor as witnessed by the Handicapped Dive Association in the USA (The Moray Wheels). There are, of course, special considerations and safety factors to be taken into account in these cases.

Among other safety considerations, divers should have a basic knowledge of the local sea conditions, underwater communications with dive buddies, and should be familiar with their diving equipment. The latter should be in good working order, and carefully checked, especially if it has been packed away for a year or more.

Although certified divers can generally rent gear and dive on their own throughout the islands, it is advisable to dive first with a local organization in order to obtain local information such as weather, tides and various local hazards.

Most organizations have full sets of equipment for hire and offer only a very small reduction in price, if one provides one's own gear. Therefore, consider carefully the merits of travelling with heavy and bulky dive equipment, if you can be assured that good quality gear is available from a local operator. However, some divers are more comfortable using their own gear.

The use of a dive flag is also important to prevent boats from coming too close to areas where divers are operating. Certified divers should be well aware of all these safety points.

For those who are not divers but are considering taking up the sport, be forewarned: it is easy to become a scuba addict, especially when exploring some of the thrilling destinations covered in this guide. So, whether you are a seasoned diver looking for new and challenging discoveries or a beginner, enjoy safe diving as you venture into this exciting world.

THE MARINE LIFE IN THE CARIBBEAN

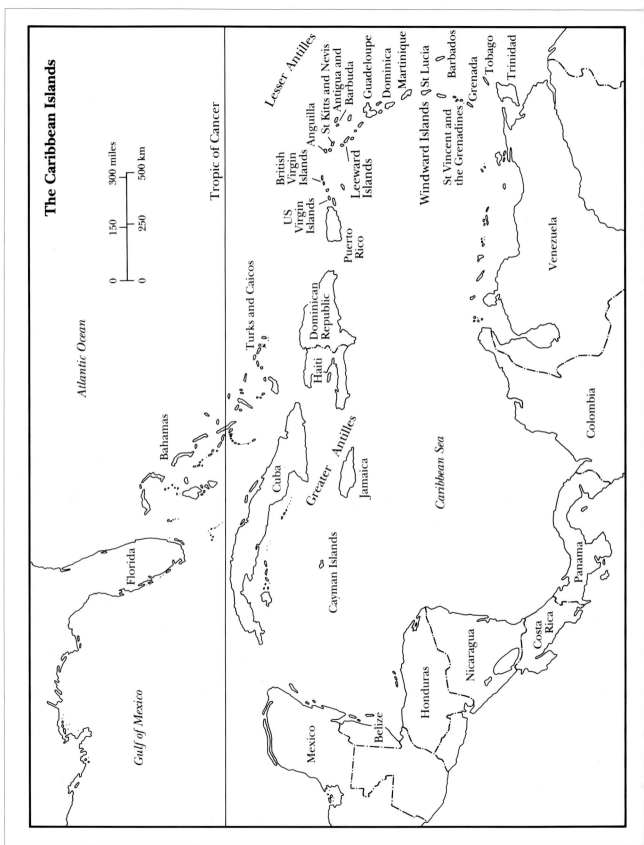

The Caribbean Islands

Atlantic Ocean

Tropic of Cancer

300 miles

500 km

150

250

0

0

Lesser Antilles

St Kitts and Nevis

Antigua and Barbuda

Guadeloupe

Dominica

Martinique

St Lucia

Barbados

Tobago

Trinidad

Grenada

Anguilla

British Virgin Islands

US Virgin Islands

Puerto Rico

Leeward Islands

Windward Islands

St Vincent and the Grenadines

Venezuela

Turks and Caicos

Dominican Republic

Haiti

Bahamas

Cuba

Greater Antilles

Jamaica

Caribbean Sea

Colombia

Florida

Cayman Islands

Gulf of Mexico

Mexico

Belize

Honduras

Nicaragua

Costa Rica

Panama

The Marine Life in the Caribbean

The marine life is one of the main reasons most people enjoy exploring the underwater environment. The vast array of fish, invertebrates and coral life is fascinating and makes each dive a unique experience and an adventure.

Throughout most of the Caribbean sea creatures such as blackbar soldierfish, pufferfish, damselfish, crabs, lobsters, anemones, and angelfish to name but a few are commonly found. However, divers will come across some very unusual features specific to each island. For example, nowhere else but in Stingray City, in the Cayman Islands, does one come across friendly, big southern sting rays in large concentrations. Nor is there another George, like the big barracuda, a well known resident on one of the wrecks off Barbados, who spends much of his day admiring his reflection in a trapped air bubble inside one of the passage ways of the ship!

It used to be popular for divers to feed to the fish whatever they could take with them (Cheese Whiz, which could be squirted out of a can was once the rage). They could thus attract various fish which they could then observe and photograph. However, it is now generally considered bad practice as it disrupts the normal chain of events. It has also proved to be harmful both to the divers who risked

Anemone

being injured by aggressive marine life and to the fish. Many resorts now have laws protecting the environment, and often nothing can be either touched or taken away. Divers should be aware of local laws and act accordingly, in agreement with the common cliche 'take only pictures, leave only bubbles'.

Underwater photography and filming is now the biggest attraction for sport divers. Most divers enjoy photographing the marine life, ship wrecks and dive buddies, learning at the same time to be more aware and more knowledgeable of the marine environment and its creatures. It must be noted, however, that underwater photography requires specialized training and that divers should be certified before they set off with often cumbersome camera equipment.

While most divers are very aware of the fish dashing about the reef, for some, especially the novice diver, there is a treasure chest of fascinating invertebrate creatures to be opened up. There are excellent reference books on this topic, one of the best being *The Reef Set* by Paul Humann. It is a series of three identification books on *Reef Fish*, *Reef Creatures* and *Reef Coral*. They are beautifully illustrated with colour photographs and very well written. Other books are advertised in all top dive publications and are a good way to begin to understand the marine world.

Non-divers or novice divers are frequently frightened of marine life without any reason. Most sea creatures act defensively and will rarely attack divers if they are not provoked. Against dangerous marine life such as members of the jelly fish family that are highly toxic (Portuguese man-of-war, sea wasp), the best defense for divers is to learn how to recognize them and how to give basic first-aid in the event of contact with one of them.

Knowing about the marine environment, its riches, its pleasures and its dangers will greatly enhance the experience of scuba diving. It is well worth spending the time, money and effort to acquire such knowledge.

Stan Waterman filming underwater

Anguilla

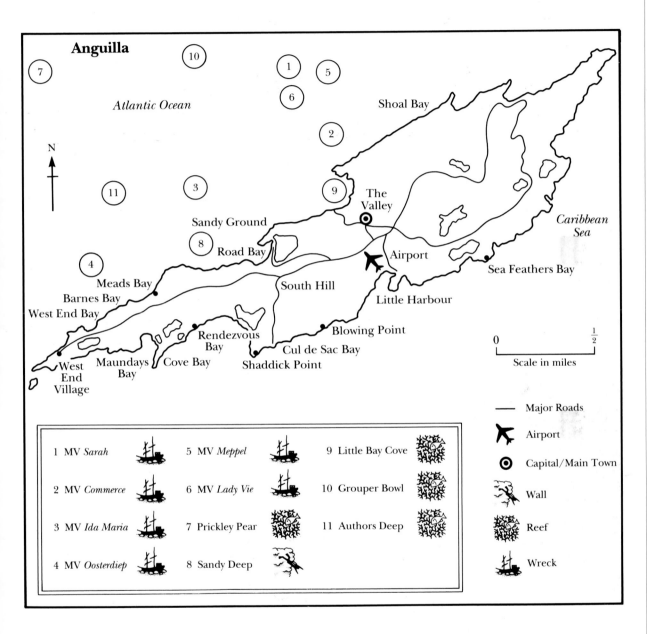

Anguilla

7

10

1

5

6

Atlantic Ocean

Shoal Bay

2

N

3

9

The Valley

Caribbean Sea

11

Sandy Ground

8   Road Bay

Airport

Sea Feathers Bay

4

Meads Bay

South Hill

Barnes Bay

Little Harbour

West End Bay

Rendezvous Bay

Blowing Point

West End Village

Maundays Bay

Cove Bay

Cul de Sac Bay

Shaddick Point

0   1/2

Scale in miles

#			#			#		
1	MV *Sarah*		5	MV *Meppel*		9	Little Bay Cove	
2	MV *Commerce*		6	MV *Lady Vie*		10	Grouper Bowl	
3	MV *Ida Maria*		7	Prickley Pear		11	Authors Deep	
4	MV *Oosterdiep*		8	Sandy Deep				

— Major Roads

✈ Airport

◉ Capital/Main Town

Wall

Reef

Wreck

Anguilla, one of the few really unspoiled Caribbean islands left, is truly the choice for the diver who does not want a crowded boat or site. An island with few divers, and only one single dive shop . . . this is still the reality on this lovely island. However one may fear that it is only a matter of time before it, too, becomes discovered.

Meanwhile, for those lucky enough to explore Anguilla while it is still unknown, there is the added excitement of exploring places few divers have seen. There indeed, one does

Aerial view of a Caribbean reef

not run the risk of diving in the company of 20 or 30 others, all dashing to the same spot dived every single day of the year.

Anguilla, located in the Eastern Caribbean, is the most northerly of the Leeward Islands and her nearest neighbour is the island of St Maarten which is half-Dutch and half-French.

Anguilla is a long flat coral island fringed with around 30 magnificent sandy beaches, said by many to be among the finest in the Caribbean. For those who seek privacy, finding a deserted beach is guaranteed. Being all coral, Anguilla provides, all around the island, excellent reef diving with very good visibility and an abundance of marine life.

Among the very many sites, one must mention in particular Sandy Island, Sandy Deep, Paintcan Reef and Prickley Pear.

Prickley Pear ranging from 30 to 70 ft is suitable both for the experienced and novice diver. Two reefs are separated by a white sand channel which provides coral overhangs, ledges and small caves in between the reef systems. Varied invertebrate and marine life abound under these colourful ledges, such as coral banded shrimp and arrow crabs. Occasional nurse sharks are tucked under the ledges and sting rays are sometimes seen lying on the sandy bottom.

Sandy Deep, off Sandy island, provides a mini-wall dive dropping from 15 to 60 ft, with a wealth of hard and soft corals and a large variety of reef fish.

Little Bay Cove is a very shallow dive (10 to 30 ft) but one is guaranteed to see shoals of literally thousands of tiny silversides swaying

Arrow crab

Grouper Bowl, 25 to 50 ft deep, is part of Sail Reef system and has some of the most spectacular hard coral formations around the island. Turtles and lobsters are usually found there.

Authors Deep, in 110 ft, is the deepest site normally dived. Black coral, not found on many islands, is abundant although no taking is allowed. Large pelagic fish like sharks and eagle rays are sometimes spotted.

However, this is not the only type of diving on offer and Anguilla provides the intrepid diver with many exciting wrecks to explore.

In the summer of 1990, the government of Anguilla, along with a US-based commercial salvage company, sank four ships around the island, adding to the two wreck diving sites already in existence.

in the water. It is an excellent site for a second dive of the day.

Diver with large black coral tree

The MV **Sarah**, which as a 222 ft freighter is the largest of the ships sunk, lies totally intact in 80 ft of water although the shallowest part, at 30 ft, can be clearly seen from the surface. The MV *Sarah* was built by the Grangemouth Dockyard Company Ltd, on the Firth of Forth, on the east coast of Scotland. Completed on 9 March 1956, she began her life as the *Gannet*, a general purpose dry cargo vessel. She was renamed *Sarah* by her second owner – in honour of his mother – and was moved to Newfoundland. In 1983, she was moved to the Caribbean where she was purchased by the Anguilla Marine Transportation Company Ltd. However, on 7 November 1984, she was hit by Hurricane Klaus and she partially sank. Finally, on 29 June 1990, as most of the island's population looked on, *Sarah* was lifted out of the water and relocated to the eastern end of the Sail Reef system.

Tamarian Water Sports, the only dive shop on Anguilla, has a detailed history of *Sarah* for those interested in more details. Common marine life around her includes rays, barracuda and schools of jacks. The superstructure left intact makes an excellent backdrop for underwater photography.

Diver with rock beauties

The MV *Commerce*, a 137 ft freighter built in Holland in 1955, lies in 45 to 80 ft of water off Flat Cap Point. Intentionally sunk in 1986, she sits intact and upright on a sloping bottom. The structure is very open and allows for divers to swim through her in complete safety. Having been down for some years, she shelters a wide variety of fish and occasionally large sting rays can be spotted.

The MV *Ida Maria*, a 119 ft freighter built around World War I and also intentionally sunk in 1985, sits upright and semi-intact in 60 ft of water. She started her life as a general cargo vessel on European trade routes until she was sold and brought to the Caribbean by Mr Clement Daniels who donated her to be sunk as a diving attraction. Although penetration of this wreck is not allowed as it is unsafe, the site affords the diver a unique interaction with marine life as the dive masters have hand-fed the marine creatures who are most approachable! One can admire large French angelfish, schools of Atlantic spadefish, rock beauties and remarkably large spotted drums. Lobsters have also made this site home. Truly, for abundant marine life and good photogenic material this site is exceptional!

Other wrecks include the MV *Oosterdiep*, lying in 80 ft off Barnes Bay, the MV *Meppel* and the MV *Lady Vie*, also lying in 80 ft. All three sites are upright and intact. Slowly, marine life is being attracted to these wrecks and turtles, spadefish, angelfish, sting rays and grunts can be regularly seen.

When one tires of diving, beach-combing is a must on Anguilla, as it has some of the most beautiful beaches to be found in the Caribbean. Double dives present the great advantage of visiting beaches which can be reached only by boat, in between dives. Among those which can be reached by car, one must mention **Rendezvous Bay**, **Cove Bay**, **Maundays Bay** and **Shoal Bay** where sparkling white sand stretches ad infinitum! On the opposite end of the island, on **Captains Bay**, breakers roll in, perfect for surfing if one so desires. It is very isolated and rather difficult to reach but well worth the effort and the journey for the adventuresome!

There is no doubt that the whole of Anguilla, both above and under water, deserves to be explored as it is one of the very few remaining places in the world left totally unspoilt.

Directory

Tamarian Watersports Ltd
Box 247
The Valley
Anguilla, British West Indies
TELEPHONE 809 497 2020   FAX 809 497 5125

• *For further information, contact:*

Anguilla Department of Tourism:
The Valley
Anguilla, British West Indies
TELEPHONE 809 497 2759   FAX 809 497 2751

USA:
Medhurst & Associates
271 Main Street
Northport, New York 11768, USA
TELEPHONE 800 553 4939

UK:
Anguilla Department of Tourism
3 Epirus Road
London, SW6 7UJ, Great Britain
TELEPHONE 071 937 7725

Antigua and Barbuda

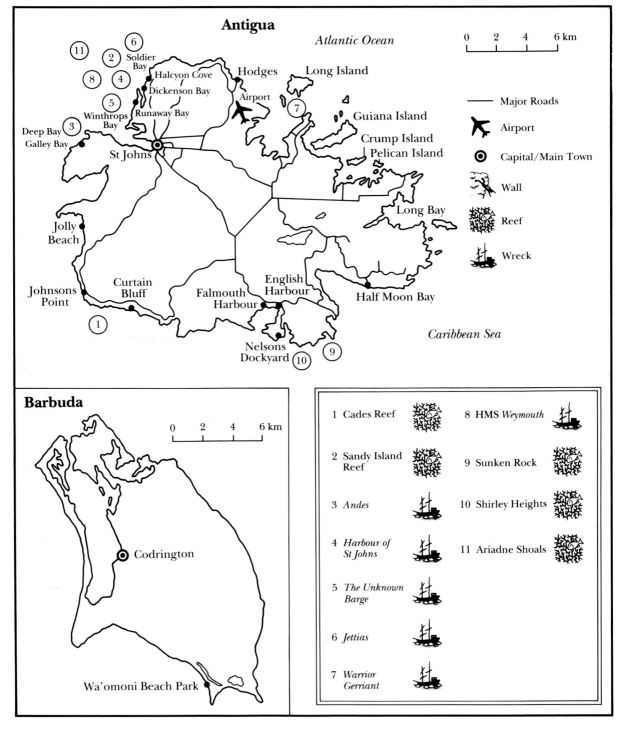

Antigua

Atlantic Ocean

0 2 4 6 km

⑪ ⑥ Soldier
   ②   Bay
⑧ ④ Halcyon Cove
       Dickenson Bay
   ⑤
Winthrops Runaway Bay
Bay
Deep Bay ③
Galley Bay
   St Johns

Hodges
Airport

Long Island

⑦

Guiana Island
Crump Island
Pelican Island

Long Bay

Jolly
Beach

Johnsons
Point

Curtain
Bluff

Falmouth
Harbour

English
Harbour

Half Moon Bay

①

Nelsons
Dockyard ⑩ ⑨

Caribbean Sea

—— Major Roads

✈ Airport

◎ Capital/Main Town

Wall

Reef

Wreck

Barbuda

0 2 4 6 km

◎ Codrington

Wa'omoni Beach Park

1 Cades Reef

2 Sandy Island
   Reef

3 *Andes*

4 *Harbour of
   St Johns*

5 *The Unknown
   Barge*

6 *Jettias*

7 *Warrior
   Gerriant*

8 HMS *Weymouth*

9 Sunken Rock

10 Shirley Heights

11 Ariadne Shoals

Around much of Antigua, the surf breaks on barrier reefs alive with colourful tropical fish. This makes for mostly shallow diving (above 60 ft) and one has to really seek out deep diving. The underwater terrain matches the topside which is very flat, as Antigua is a coral island. It is said that 1000 square miles of coral reef surround Antigua and Barbuda. However, Antigua offers a wide range of sites from the easily accessible reef dives, to wrecks and deeper and more difficult sites for the experienced diver.

One of the better and easily accessible sites is **Cades Reef**, a 2½ mile reef running along the leeward coast of the island. The reef is still virginal and part of it has been established as an underwater park. It is to be hoped, therefore, that it will remain a top diving site for years to come. Cades Reef often offers a 80 to 100 ft visibility – sometimes up to 150 ft – which is what one expects in the clear, warm Caribbean waters. Most of the shops in Antigua will schedule dives to Cades Reef and have their own sites but, as the reef is so extensive, there are unlimited locations available. Among them one must include **Eel Run**, **Snapper Ledge**, **Big Sponge** and **The Chimney**, whose evocative names speak for themselves. Fish life abounds, with parrot fish

Stylaster roseus (a delicate pink coral)

providing a rainbow of colours amidst the staghorn coral that readily grows on the shallow reefs. Schools of blue tang and masses of small harmless barracuda are easily seen.

Sandy Island Reef, on the leeward coast, a short 15 minutes boat ride from the nearest dive shop, is the favourite site for two of the shops nearby. The reef is covered in a variety of corals and gorgonia which the diver can explore either in shallow water (30 ft only) or along the edge of the reef, fringed by a white sand bottom, in 50 ft of water. Life abounds, with parrot fish dashing amidst the ever-present staghorn coral.

Antigua offers some wreck diving, although as some of the wrecks are badly broken up, it can be a bit of a disappointment to those expecting an intact ship filled with gold! One of the shops actually discourages dives to the wrecks as they can be a let down. However, for the serious wreck diver, some of the old sites are well worth a visit.

Among them are the *Andes*, in Deep Bay, lying in only 20 ft of water, and the *Harbour of St Johns*, a 90 ft steel tug which sank in St Johns harbour while the water pump was being repaired. This same pump is still held in the vice in 40 ft of water where she now rests, just outside Deep Bay.

About 60 ft behind the *Harbour of St Johns*, and 20 ft to the left, one can find the remains of an old barge, known locally as *The Unknown Barge*. Although nothing is known of her past, her present provides a home for a school of small reef fish!

The steamship *Jettias*, which sank around 1917 as she was departing for the UK, lies in shallow water (about 24 ft) off Diamond Bank, and the *Warrior Gerriant* is just off Maiden Island, although she is badly broken up.

The wreck of the HMS *Weymouth* after which the reef of Sandy Island is named, was carrying missionaries to South America in the 1700s when it went to ground. Although the ship's carpenter insisted they abandon ship, the missionaries maintained she would not sink. Thus, all but the carpenter remained on board and perished.

There are three or four other wrecks around Weymouth Reef and Sandy Island, and anchors and cannon can be spotted in various locations! As the wrecks of Antigua vary in size, depth and in the marine life surrounding them, one can choose the type one wishes to explore.

The third type of site Antigua provides is that of deep diving suitable for the more experienced diver only. Two of these are particularly spectacular.

Sunken Rock is truly exceptional, with a maximum depth of 122 ft, which is very unusual in Antigua's waters. Along the drop-off of the rock ledge, one may see magnificent open water fish (sting rays, large barracuda and maybe even a dolphin or two). The rock forms a cleft allowing divers to swim through. This gives the sensation of a cave dive as one glides along under a few coral overhangs, between the cleft of the large coral formations, without the dangers of cave diving as the diver is always in open water and can easily surface. The main danger is the depth which must be monitored to stay within safe decompression time. Once the sandy bottom is reached, a gentle ascent can be made along the outside of the coral formation, until one is on a typical tropical coral reef, in 40 ft of water, among blue and brown chromis, sergeant major protecting their territory, and the numerous parrot fish which are always in residence.

Diver with colourful sponge

Diver looks in coral cave (Ariadne Shoals – Antigua)

As only one shop dives this site on a regular basis, it is advisable to confirm this destination if such a dive appeals.

Shirley Heights is another spectacular site whose depth of up to 110 ft will appeal to those seeking deeper dives. Coral overhangs provide homes for an abundance of small reef fish and colourful sponges. In addition, one sees rays, turtles, tiger groupers and the occasional shark gliding by. Schools of spade fish are also spotted around this site. Because of its location only two of the dive shops regularly visit this area.

Last, but certainly not least of the dive sites off Antigua is **Ariadne Shoals**, a mile-long reef, located 11.31 nautical miles to sea on the southwest of the island. Although it is about an hour's boat ride, sometimes in rough seas, once on the site the diver has something really exciting to look forward to. Discovered from the air, this site was, until recent years, virtually unexplored. Even now, only one dive shop, Dive Antigua, regularly dives it. Its owner, Big John, a veteran operator on Antigua, is very conservation minded and will not allow anything to be disturbed. The marine life is indeed amazingly prolific. During one of a recent double dive, the author and her fellow divers came across six large nurse sharks (about six to eight feet) which they were able to stroke gently! In addition, pompano jacks, remoras, pairs of graceful French angels, schools of colourful French grunts and large lobsters were sighted, to name but a few! Exit and entry onto the boat can be tricky in choppy seas, so this is not a dive for the inexperienced diver.

Diving on Antigua is easy to arrange, with several well established shops in different parts of the island. The oldest shop has been around for over 15 years. Although all shops organize dives on most of the sites mentioned, some special arrangements need to be made for some of them. For the non-diver, instruction is available.

Barbuda is the delightful 'little sister island' of Antigua and the waters surrounding this tiny gem are totally unexplored. However, the facilities are greatly limited, so, unless one is on a boat with gear and a compressor (which are not readily available), diving in Barbuda can be difficult. Occasionally, local fishermen who dive can arrange to accommodate certified divers, but this is not a structured and reliable arrangement. Like on Antigua, the water is very shallow and one can enjoy some lovely snorkelling.

During the winter months (November to April) visibility is at its best, although the sea is calmer in the summer when the trade winds die. Ground swells caused by the change of wind due to the heavy cold air coming from North America, develop around Christmas and can cause problems.

It must be noted that the water visibility overall in Antigua can be somewhat poorer than that on some well known Caribbean islands. This is due to the large shelf and vast shallow reef surrounding the island. The bright tropical sunlight and rich nutrients can lead to a mass of plankton which inhibits vis-ibility. However, it also promotes a rich coral coverage and an abundance of reef life.

There are laws for the protection of marine life that divers should observe. Lobsters, for instance, cannot be taken if under 9 inches long. Most of the shops do not allow taking of any marine life and will advise divers of this. As one shop owner commented: 'Divers can shoot anything they want, as long as they use a camera'.

This strict policy ensures that the next time one dives off Antigua, all the marine creatures will still be there.

Directory

Note: This is not an exhaustive list of all diving operators on the island.

Aquanaut Diving Center
Box 62
St Johns, Antigua
Located at St James Club
TELEPHONE 809 460 5000   FAX 809 460 3015

Dive Runaway
Box 874
St Johns, Antigua
Located at Runaway Beach Club
TELEPHONE 809 462 2626   FAX 809 462 3484

Dive Antigua
Box 251
St Johns, Antigua
Located at Halcyon Cove Hotel
TELEPHONE 809 462 3483   FAX 809 462 7787

Jolly Dive
Box 744
St Johns, Antigua
Located at Jolly Beach Hotel
TELEPHONE 809 462 0061/0068
FAX 809 462 1827

Dockyard Divers
Box 184
St Johns, Antigua
Located at Nelsons Dockyard
TELEPHONE 809 460 1178   FAX 809 460 1179

Pirate Divers
Box 155
St Johns, Antigua
Located at Lord Nelsons Beach Hotel
TELEPHONE 809 462 3094   FAX 809 462 0751

The following shops cater only to certified divers and to guests of their respective hotels.

Curtain Bluff Dive Shop
Box 288
St Johns, Antigua
Located at Curtain Bluff Hotel
TELEPHONE 809 463 1115/11169

Long Bay Dive Shop
Box 442
St Johns, Antigua
Located at Long Bay Hotel
TELEPHONE 809 463 2005

• *For further information, contact:*

The Antigua and Barbuda Board of Tourism
Location: Thames Street, St Johns
Box 363
St Johns, Antigua
TELEPHONE 809 462 0480

USA:
610 Fifth Avenue,
Suite 311,
New York,
New York 10020
TELEPHONE 212 541 4117

UK:
Antigua House,
15 Thayer Street,
London W1M 5LD
TELEPHONE 071 486 7073/5
FAX 071 486 9970

Barbados

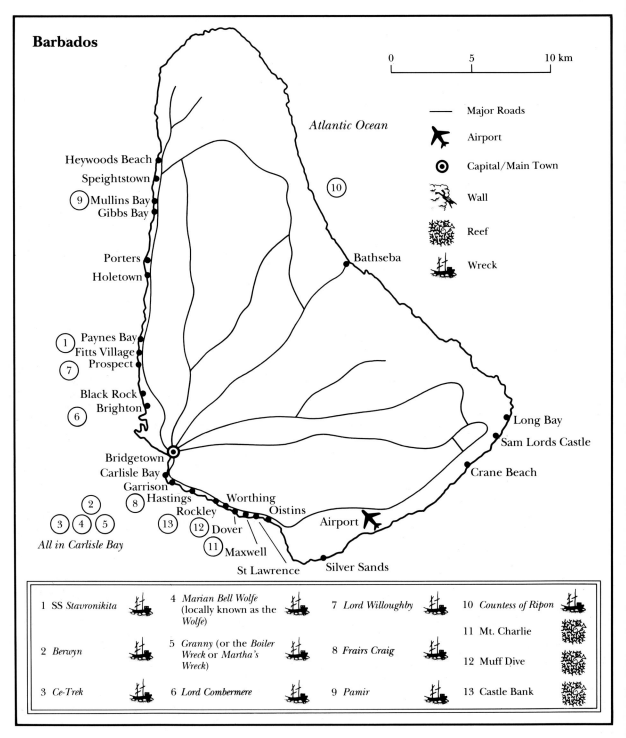

Barbados

0   5   10 km

— Major Roads

✈ Airport

◉ Capital/Main Town

Wall

Reef

Wreck

Atlantic Ocean

Heywoods Beach
Speightstown
⑨ Mullins Bay
Gibbs Bay

⑩

Porters
Holetown

Bathseba

① Paynes Bay
Fitts Village
⑦ Prospect

Black Rock
Brighton
⑥

Long Bay
Sam Lords Castle

Bridgetown
Carlisle Bay
Garrison
② ⑧ Hastings
Rockley Worthing
③ ④ ⑤ ⑬ ⑫ Dover Oistins
All in Carlisle Bay ⑪ Maxwell
St Lawrence Silver Sands

Crane Beach

Airport

1 SS *Stavronikita*	4 *Marian Bell Wolfe* (locally known as the *Wolfe*)	7 *Lord Willoughby*	10 *Countess of Ripon*
2 *Berwyn*	5 *Granny* (or the *Boiler Wreck* or *Martha's Wreck*)	8 *Frairs Craig*	11 Mt. Charlie
3 *Ce-Trek*	6 *Lord Combermere*	9 *Pamir*	12 Muff Dive
			13 Castle Bank

Barbados, one of the more developed and sophisticated islands of the Eastern Caribbean, has much to offer the visitor, apart from scuba diving. It is therefore a good choice for those who wish to do something else beside diving or who come with a companion who is not keen on the sport. If exploring the island itself, enjoying local food and night life or discovering some of its English history appeal, then Barbados is an ideal choice.

Until recently, little attention was given to the conservation of the reefs. Pollution, dynamiting by fishermen, selling of coral souvenirs, and other thoughtless human acts, caused much damage and some of the reef life is not as unspoiled as on other islands, although there are still some healthy reefs which have survived the carelessness of man.

As an attractive alternative to reef diving, Barbados has a number of interesting wrecks to explore. Several of them have been sunk intentionally as diving sites.

To the average person, the thought of wreck diving may conjure up visions of deep, dark shapes, lurking below the surface of the sea, waiting to grasp anything that violates its menacing bulk. However, to the passionate wreck diver, it evokes the excitement of mysterious discoveries. To the underwater photographer, it provides unlimited photographic opportunities.

The largest, and possibly the best known, wreck off Barbados is the SS **Stavronikita**, a 356 ft Greek cargo ship. She is among one of the largest ships intentionally sunk for divers in the Caribbean. The 'Stav' as she is called by those who know her, was built in Denmark in 1956. She first sailed under the name of *Hoio*, but changed to *Vasia* in 1971, according to

Martha Watkins Gilkes explores the 'Stavronikita' (GEORGE HUME)

the Lloyds Registry of Shipping, in London. Later renamed the *Stavronikita*, she carried cargo throughout the world until 26 August 1976, when she caught fire off Barbados, while transporting cement. The fire started at about 6 am in the Chief Engineer's cabin and swept through the ship. When it finally abated, six men were dead and another three injured. As she was drifting, two Barbados tugs came to her rescue, the *Barbados* and the *Culpepper*, on 1 September and towed her charred remains back to Barbados. Ironically, these same two tugs would eventually tow her to her final resting place where she now lies in some 130 ft of water!

After two years of debate on her fate, she was bought by the Barbados Tourist Board to be sunk as a diving site in the Barbados Marine Reserve, an underwater park protected by legislation from destruction or damage by careless divers. In such a safe place, it was felt that the *Stav* could grow into a thing of beauty for dives of the future.

Thus, on 22 November 1978, about 400 yards off the west coast of Barbados, near Prospect (St James), she was dynamited with some 200 lb of explosives which had been carefully placed at strategic points by a US Navy team from Puerto Rico. At approximately 12.35 pm, with onlookers lining the beaches, the first explosion went off. The *Stav* immediately began to sink as planned, on her keel, and six explosions later, it was all over . . . it had only taken 13 minutes and 3 seconds for her to go down. She now sits upright, only to be viewed by scuba divers!

However, she is not a forgotten lady. In addition to the countless divers who visit her on a regular basis, she has been written up in numerous magazines and, in 1980, became the subject of a documentary film by the famous American cinematographer Stan Waterman. Her 'sea life' has indeed turned her into a beauty to behold, with black coral trees adorning her decks and schools of colourful reef fish making her their home. It is however in the more shallow depths that the main growth of marine life is to be found as the deeper water and restricted sun life do not encourage it.

Her enormous size – gross tonnage of 4 129 tons – and the excellent condition of her superstructure, make her a real dream for the divers and underwater photographers.

The 'Stavronikita' on the day of her sinking (Barbados)

A friendly moray

Martha Watkins Gilkes at a port hole of the 'Stav'
(GEORGE HUME)

The *Stav* has four large cargo holds to explore and the massive main mast and derrick support ascend from the top deck in about 75 ft of water to within 15 ft of the surface. She originally had 12 winches and 14 cargo derricks, and although some of the machinery was stripped off, much was left intact. The main propeller still attached is a luring attraction, although it is in deep water (125 ft).

The *Stav* harbours one unique inhabitant locally known as George, the dancing barracuda. Over four feet long, George took up residence some years ago, but has, in recent times, adopted a new and extraordinary behaviour. He hangs vertically at 95 ft within a narrow passage way admiring his reflection in a large air bubble, caused by the accumulation of divers' exhaled air. This bubble trapped in the ceiling acts as a mirror and attracts George. One of the dive shops says that he lost his mate just before beginning this unusual behaviour. It is believed that he thinks that his reflection is his mate! The diving establishment promotes the protection of the barracuda from careless divers who attempt to pull his tail or to touch him. Although attacks on man by a barracuda are very rare – barracuda consider us too big to eat – it should be remembered that their teeth are a defensive weapon and should George feel threatened, he might well use them. He should be approached with caution and respect. No one knows how long he will carry on behaving as he does, and one can only hope that George will continue to feel at home on the *Stav*, giving divers a unique opportunity to view a barracuda at close range.

Finally, one must issue a word of warning about the *Stav*: she lies in deep water and is rated as an advanced dive, unsafe for the inexperienced diver. However, for those capable of such a dive, she is a must on a trip to Barbados. Most of the shops on the island will organize dives to this site, although, as they may not be on a daily basis, it is advisable to make arrangements in advance to avoid disappointment.

Another wreck site, and one which is easy to dive, is that of the **Berwyn**, located in Carlisle Bay. The *Berwyn* is a World War I French tug, about 50 ft long, and is totally encrusted in coral, having sunk in 1919. She lies in only 22 ft of water, and, with the top deck being only about 10 ft from the surface, she constitutes an ideal snorkelling site too. Much of the upper structure is broken up as she lies in shallow water and wave action continually causes damage. In addition, inconsiderate boaters who drop their anchors nearby have done much damage to the structure too. However, the presence of schools of hungry sergeant majors and yellow snappers always looking for a hand-out from the divers is a great attraction. Being a very easy shallow dive, and accessible either from the beach or from a boat, the *Berwyn* makes an ideal site for beginners or for that first dive of the year after a long break . . .

In February 1987, the **Ce-Trek**, 45 ft long, was sunk just south of the *Berwyn* in 40 ft of water. Only a 5 minute swim separates both wrecks which divers can therefore explore on one single dive. The *Ce-Trek* was a Barbados based fishing boat. She sank in the Carenage where she lay for two weeks before being lifted and moved to her present location. She is a concrete boat which has attracted much growth. The wooden cabin is slowly deteriorating but the main structure remains intact. A family of lobsters shelter on her leeward side.

Carlisle Bay offers three other known wrecks although a study of the local archives reveals that there are at least 12 others in the bay which used to be the original anchorage for the island. These ships are just waiting to be discovered by some lucky divers!

The **Marian Bell Wolfe**, locally known as the *Wolfe*, lies in 40 ft of water to the north of the *Berwyn*. A wooden ship built in Nova Scotia, she sailed around the waters of Saba as well as plying the waters between Guyana and Barbados. In her later days, she spent her time around the Southern Caribbean and in September 1955 she was damaged by Hurricane Janet. She eventually sank at anchor in Carlisle Bay where she is to be found. Although rather broken up and maybe not quite as interesting to some as better preserved wrecks, she does attract schools of fish.

The **Granny**, also called the **Boiler Wreck**, known locally as **Martha's Wreck**, lies in 45 ft of water to the north of the *Wolfe*. It is said that she was transferring drums of gasoline to another vessel, when an explosion sank her. Only a part of her metal structure is still visible, but what there is affords an array of rich marine life, with a very large green moray as resident. Turtles can often be spotted and divers have also seen manta rays gracefully gliding by . . . a real underwater treat.

Carlisle Bay presents an added attraction to the diver; it is a marvelous hunting ground for antique bottles. As the bay was the anchorage for seventeenth and eighteenth century ships, a profusion of bottles are waiting to be discovered: wine bottles of different ages and types, assorted stoneware, mineral water bottles of various shapes and marble bottles. Since Barbados was British until the 1960s, many of these bottles are of British origin. Thus, an authoritative book on antique bottles would be a welcome addition to a Barbados diving holiday!

Martha Watkins Gilkes on 'Frairs Craig'
(GEORGE HUME)

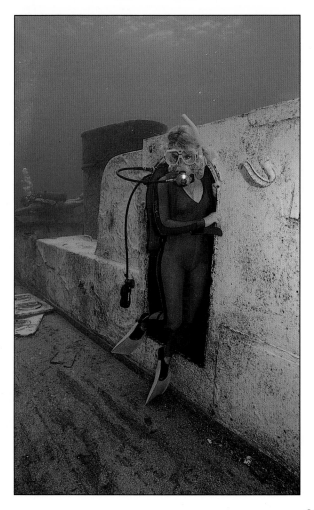

Up the west coast of the island, *Lord Combermere* and *Lord Willoughby* rest. **Lord Combermere** is a metal tug boat which was intentionally sunk around 1974. Some say that she was a water tender to a larger boat. Locally she is called the **Shallow Wreck**, as she sits upright on a slope that falls gently from 30 to 50 ft, off Black Rock. The hold is easily accessible through an opening on her deck. As an added treat to exploring her, one has the opportunity to observe a school of graceful garden eels, swaying in the current just off the propeller on the nearby sandy 60 ft bottom.

Lord Willoughby, probably so named after a former governor of the island, is also an old water barge, approximately 60 ft long. She too was sunk intentionally around 1975. She is located next to Clarkes Reef which is in about 60 ft water. Lying in about 100 ft of water, she is just off the reef.

July 1985 saw two new names added onto the list of the wrecks of Barbados: the *Frairs Craig* and *Pamir*.

The **Frairs Craig** was a 160 ft long, 590 ton freighter built in Holland in 1938. In the 1970s, she sat at anchor, unused, in Carlisle Bay for about ten years. Eventually, the Barbados Port Authorities decided that she was a hazard to other ships in the bay, as her anchor chain had rusted to the point of being unsafe. The decision was taken to sink her, with the consent of her owner, and on 2 July 1985, she came to rest in 50 ft of water on a sandy bottom at latitude 13° 04' on the south coast of Barbados, just outside Carlisle Bay. She is fringed on the shore side by a 30 ft reef and on the starboard side by a 60 ft reef. Before she was sunk, holes had been cut in her sides to enable divers to swim safely inside the hull. The mast and crane boom had been cut and secured to the hatch. Most of the engine room was left intact and the propeller remains. When she went down, there was already ten years of growth on her propeller, from her long anchorage, making it a superb

Martha Watkins Gilkes on 'Frairs Craig' (GEORGE HUME)

site for photographers. Since then, some wave action has damaged the structure, but, although she has actually broken up, she remains an interesting site, especially as one can incorporate a shallow reef dive in one's dive plan.

The **Pamir**, a 150 ft motor vessel was sunk off the west coast of Barbados on 19 July 1985. She went down in 50 ft of water, in just 15 minutes, after her sea cocks were opened. Schools of blue chromis and blackbar soldierfish congregate within her structure and, like the *Stav*, she too is undergoing a 'Sea Change' turning into an object of beauty for divers to enjoy.

The wrecks aforementioned are all twentieth century ships, however, as is true with all the Caribbean islands, tales abound of

Martha Watkins Gilkes on 'Pamir'
(GEORGE HUME)

ancient wrecks, perhaps with treasure still on board! Every diver dreams of finding a gold-laden ship. While no one can boast of this yet, it must be said that there are records of over 70 wrecks sinking between 1666 and 1872 in the waters off Barbados, 12 of them in Carlisle Bay and most of the remainder on the east coast of the island.

One such ancient wreck was mentioned by Mr Edward Stoute, a well known Barbadian historian, in a newspaper article, on 20 June 1976. According to Mr Stoute, a steamer known as **Cuban Wreck** broke her propeller shaft while entering Carlisle Bay in 1872 and sank. No one can determine the exact location where she lies, but, some day, a lucky diver may well stumble upon her adding yet

another name to the list of Barbadian wreck sites.

The famed Sam Lord of Barbados is reputed to have hung lanterns in the coconut trees off his castle, on the rough east coast of the island, to lure ships onto the shallow reefs before proceding to loot them. He may, however, be blamed for more than he deserves. During the time he occupied the castle (now a hotel) from 1820 to 1844, only nine ships are reported to have sunk on Cobblers Reef, which is situated directly off the castle.

Another nineteenth century ship wreck lies on the east coast, but few know the location. The **Countess of Ripon** sank in 1866, when she hit a reef off Skeets Bay. She was a new iron ship of 1209 tons, coming from India to St Vincent. Today, her brass bell can be seen at the Barbados Turf Club – a tribute to the memory of this sailing lady of the past.

For many ancient wrecks, however, nothing but a note in the archives attest their existence.

Although much emphasis has been placed so far on wreck diving, which is unquestionably the aspect most developed on Barbados, there are a number of reefs worth diving around the island.

Mt. Charlie, on the south coast, is home for beautiful large sponges (orange elephant ear, tube sponge, for example) as well as black coral and other live coral formations. Sea fans and gorgonians enhance the sloping reef that drops to 180 ft. Being still totally unspoiled, this 75 ft deep reef was chosen in 1991 by the Eastern Caribbean Safe Diving Association (ECSDA) to be the site of a permanent mooring to help protect the coral from anchor damage.

The **Muff Dive**, a narrow reef that begins at around 60 ft and slopes to 180 ft, draws pelagic fish and turtles. There can be swells on this site, so it is not recommended for beginners unless the weather is particularly calm.

Recompression chamber in Barbados (TONY GILKES)

Castle Bank Reef, also on the south coast, runs parallel to shore and begins at 60 ft, dropping to around 80 ft. Gorgonia, large sponges, brain and lettuce coral adorn its sides.

These are only some of the numerous coral reefs around Barbados. The dive operators on the island have their favourite sites for the diver to choose from.

Diving in Barbados is much safer than on some other Caribbean destinations. The island has a recompression chamber which is used for treating diving accidents. It is owned and operated by the Barbados Defense Force with assistance from the ECSDA.

As was mentioned in the opening chapter to this guide, the ECSDA is a voluntary organization which helped raise funds to install the chamber in 1985. It has also established minimum safe operating standards for diving shops on the island. Barbados is among the first of the Leeward and Windward Islands to possess such safety standards. The system is a self-imposed one and not all diving establishments adhere to it. It is extremely advisable to check which shops are safety minded before planning a diving vacation with them.

Safety, quality, extensive wreck sites, a variety of entertainment and tourist facilities outside scuba diving make Barbados a very appealing choice to those who want more than just dive.

Directory

Please note that this is not an exhaustive list of all dive operators in Barbados, but a cross-section of some of the more established and safety minded shops.

The Dive Shop, Ltd.
Box 44B
St Michael
Barbados
TELEPHONE 809 426 9947

Exploresub Barbados
Christ Church
St Lawrence Gap
Barbados
TELEPHONE 809 435 6542   FAX 809 428 4674

Underwater Barbados
Coconut Court
Hastings
Christ Church
Barbados
TELEPHONE 809 426 0655   FAX 809 429 8198

Willies Water Sports
Philmara House
3 Porters
St James
Barbados
TELEPHONE/FAX 809 422 1834

Dive Boat Safari
c/o Barbados Hilton
Needhams Point
Barbados
TELEPHONE 809 427 4350

Blue Reef Watersports
Glitter Bay
St James
Barbados
TELEPHONE 809 422 3133

• *For further information, contact:*

The Barbados Board of Tourism
Box 242
Harbour Road
Bridgetown
Barbados
TELEPHONE 809 427 2626

USA:
800 Second Avenue
New York, New York 10017
TELEPHONE 212 986 6516/800 221 9831
FAX 212 573 9850

UK:
Barbados Board of Tourism
663 Tottenham Court Road
London W1P 9AA
TELEPHONE 071 636 9448/9

The British Virgin Islands

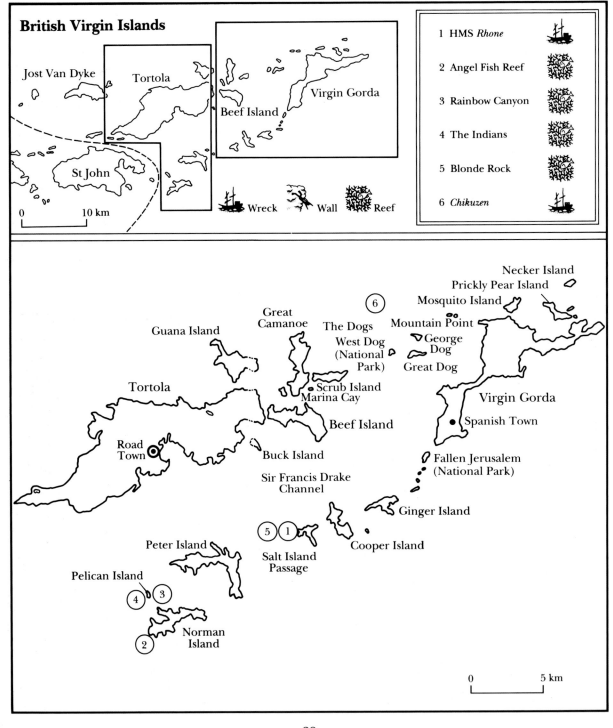

British Virgin Islands

Jost Van Dyke

Tortola

St John

0   10 km

Beef Island

Virgin Gorda

Wreck   Wall   Reef

1 HMS *Rhone*

2 Angel Fish Reef

3 Rainbow Canyon

4 The Indians

5 Blonde Rock

6 *Chikuzen*

Necker Island
Prickly Pear Island
Mosquito Island
Mountain Point
⑥
George
Dog
Great Dog

Great
Camanoe

The Dogs
West Dog
(National
Park)

Guana Island

Tortola

Scrub Island
Marina Cay

Beef Island

Virgin Gorda

Spanish Town

Road
Town

Buck Island

Sir Francis Drake
Channel

Fallen Jerusalem
(National Park)

Ginger Island

⑤ ①

Salt Island
Passage

Cooper Island

Peter Island

Pelican Island

④ ③

②   Norman
Island

0   5 km

The British Virgin Islands boast some of the best diving in the Caribbean, with an array of 50 coral islands, scattered over a wide area, surrounded by reef. Even so, the sheer number of diving sites is not what makes the BVIs so special. Unlike some other islands in the Caribbean, the BVIs are conservation minded and are well aware of the valuable resource they have in the marine environment which is carefully protected in many ways. For example, it is forbidden to remove any marine life without a permit. The islands are also establishing permanent moorings for boats in an effort to stop the dropping of anchors on live coral. The diving industry is flourishing, well organized and very safety conscious, with first rate shops which make for easy and safe diving.

The best known site is the HMS **Rhone**, a 310 ft ocean steamer which sank under the command of a Captain Wooley, during a hurricane in 1867. She was made famous by the Columbia Pictures movie, *The Deep*, based on Peter Benchley's story of treasure diving. To dive on a ship which has been down for over 120 years and is covered with invertebrate life and a wealth of fish, is a particularly thrilling experience.

The *Rhone* lies in the 798 acre Rhone Marine Park, designed to ensure her a safe future. As the depth at the site varies from 15 ft to 80 ft, divers of all levels can enjoy it. She is usually dived as a double dive, with the deeper section explored first. She is a photographer's paradise as orange tubastrea and colourful sponges cover the structure.

In September 1989, Hurricane Hugo uncovered bones from the *Rhone*. These remains were brought up and buried on Salt Island, where a plaque reads 'A hurricane sent me down, a hurricane brought me up'. All shops

The wreck of the 'Rhone' (BVIs)

in the BVIs know the wreck very well and give excellent tours.

Another unique wreck site, although much more recent, is that of the **Chikuzen**, a 246 ft steel hull long line fishing boat which spent her final days as a cold storage facility, tied up alongside a dock in St Martin. In September 1981, as her engines no longer operated, she had to be removed from the dock and taken to sea to be sunk. Her cocks were opened, but, reluctant to sink, she drifted some 70 miles until she eventually went down at her present location, in the Sir Francis Drake Channel. She lies in 75 ft of water on her port side on a sandy bottom nearly 10 miles out to sea from Virgin Gorda. She has attracted large marine life such as large (200 lb) groupers, schools of horse eye jacks and barracuda and even the occasional shark. The top deck rests at 40 ft and her hull is covered with thorny oyster shells and a variety of marine life. Because of her location, she is best dived in calm seas, and even then, it takes over an hour to reach the site. However, she is an exciting wreck for the more experienced diver.

The waters of the BVIs are rich in marine life, and myriads of reef fish, sting rays, eagle rays, turtles and even manta can often be spotted in various reef sites.

Among them, two are particularly worth mentioning, **Angel Fish Reef**, off Norman Island, and **Rainbow Canyon**, off Pelican Island (just off Norman Island). Both sites feature coral and rock overhangs with vibrant yellow and purple fairy bassets hiding underneath. **Angel Fish Reef** slopes from 30 to 90 ft and the underwater rocky ridges form narrow canyons and channels covered with coral growth, one can swim through.

Rainbow Canyon, often used for novice divers and check out dives for beginners ranges from 15 ft to about 50 ft and offers a variety of small marine life.

Stan Waterman with a large Nassau grouper

French angelfish

The **Indians** is a dramatic formation of four massive rocks, west of Pelican Island, which rise above the water from a depth of 50 ft. It features a unique small cave, between two rocks, which, being filled with coopers sweepers, makes a beautiful photo setting. There is also a 15 ft long and 5 ft wide tunnel through which divers can pass easily.

Blonde Rock is an underwater pinnacle, situated in the mid-channel between Dead Chest and Salt Island, near the wreck of the *Rhone*. It derives its name from the massive coverage of fire coral over the top of the rocks. Starting at 15 ft it drops to an sandy bottom at 60 ft. As one descends, one can admire overhangs, ledges and small caves covered in orange and yellow cup corals. These recesses provide a natural home for schools of cooper and glassy sweepers, blackbar soldierfish and squirrelfish. Invertebrate life is also in abundance.

Painted Walls, **Alice in Wonderland**, and **The Aquarium** are just a few of other well known diving locations. The names are as varied as the choice of sites. Indeed, one dive shop boasts over 50 different underwater tours ranging from 10 to 130 ft deep!

Anegada, the most secluded island, is famous for many old wrecks scattered on the reefs. Diving is still virginal and not easy to arrange. In fact, because of the great number of ship wrecks, the Department of Fisheries may put temporary restrictions on anchoring in the area. This should be checked before attempting to dive in Anegada.

The sites which have been mentioned are only a small selection of the very many available on the BVIs.

It must also be noted that, beside first rate land based diving operations offered throughout the BVIs, Tortola is also the home base for some live-aboard dive boats which vary in size and can accommodate from a handful of divers to a large number. For those who wish to be positioned at all times over a site, this is an excellent option.

Whatever the choice one makes, the British Virgin Islands' diving is something not to be missed by the serious scuba diver.

Directory

Please note that the following is a list of some of the established dive operators. It may not contain every scuba diving operator in the BVIs.

Baskin' in the Sun
Prospect Reef Resort
West End, Long Bay
Box 108
Roadtown, Tortola, BVI
TELEPHONE 809 494 2858   FAX 809 494 3288

Blue Waters Divers
Nanny Cay Resort and Marina
Box 846
Roadtown, Tortola, BVI
TELEPHONE 809 494 2847   FAX 809 494 3288

Caribbean Images Tours
(snorkelling trips only)
Box 75
Roadtown, Tortola, BVI
TELEPHONE 809 495 2563

Dive BVI Ltd
Box 1040
Virgin Gorda, BVI
TELEPHONE 809 495 5513/7328
FAX 809 495 5347

Island Diver Ltd
Village Cay Marina
Box 3023
Roadtown, Tortola, BVI
TELEPHONE 809 494 2746

Kilbrides Underwater Tours
Box 40
Virgin Gorda, BVI
TELEPHONE 809 496 0111   FAX 809 494 2756

Underwater Safaris
Moorings Resort Dock
Box 139
Roadtown, Tortola, BVI
TELEPHONE 809 494 3235   FAX 809 494 2756

• Live aboard dive boats

Cuan Law
Trimarine Boat Company
Box 362
Roadtown, Tortola, BVI
TELEPHONE 809 648 3393   FAX 809 494 5774
800 494 2490

La Buscadsora
Box 3069
Roadtown, Tortola, BVI
TELEPHONE 809 494 3623

Promenada
Box 3100
Roadtown, Tortola, BVI
TELEPHONE 809 494 3853

• For further information, contact:

BVI Tourist Board
Box 134
Roadtown, Tortola, BVI
TELEPHONE 809 494 3134

USA:
370 Lexington Avenue, Suite 511
New York, New York 10017
TELEPHONE 212 696 0400

UK:
BVI Information Office
Great Eastern Hotel, Suite 338
London EC2M 7QN
TELEPHONE 071 283 4130   FAX 071 283 4132

• Additional reading:

MARLER, GEROGE and LUANA (1978). *The Royal Mail Steamer Rhone.* Marler Publications Ltd.
SORENSEN, L (1992). *Diving and Snorkelling Guide to the British Virgin Islands.* Pisces Books.

The Cayman Islands

The diving in the Cayman Islands is the most developed of all the Caribbean Islands. They claim to have over 1000 different sites and more than 180 instructors who are members of the Cayman Islands Watersports Operators Association! Statistics say that in excess of 50 000 divers visit the island annually.

This of course means that one is more likely to be diving from a large boat with numerous others, and exploring reefs which are dived on daily. There are, though, many positive aspects to such a developed location.

Unlike most of the islands, there is a strict code of conduct and safety with which operators must comply. There is also the added safety factor of the availability of a recompression chamber. A high priority is given to the conservation and protection of the environment and there is something for everyone, in terms of the accommodation and dive site, and the type of diving and dive operation.

Due to the tremendous popularity of diving in the Cayman Islands, there are at least two excellent guides which give extensive details of the sites throughout the Caymans. For this reason, while it is unthinkable not to mention such a diving mecca in this guide, it was decided not to try to cover specific dive sites as it would be impossible to better what has already been done. Please refer to the Directory at the end of this chapter for details of these two guides.

Directory

The large number of dive operators in the Cayman Islands, makes it impossible to list them all. Following is a selection of some of the recommended shops. A complete listing is available from the Department of Tourism.

Bob Sotos Diving
(Owner) Ron Kipp
Box 1801
Grand Cayman BWI
TELEPHONE 809 949 7700   800 262 7686

Brac Aquatics
Box 89
Cayman Brac BWI
TELEPHONE 809 948 7429

Don Fosters Dive Cayman Ltd
Box 151
Grand Cayman BWI
TELEPHONE 809 947 5132   800 83 DIVER

Parrots Landing Watersports Park
Box 1995
Grand Cayman BWI
TELEPHONE 809 949 7884   800 448 0428

Peter Milburns Dive Cayman
Box 595
Grand Cayman BWI
TELEPHONE 809 947 4341

Red Sail Sports
Box 1588
Grand Cayman BWI
TELEPHONE 809 947 5965   800 255 6425

Sunset Divers
Box 479
Grand Cayman BWI
TELEPHONE 809 949 7111   800 854 4767

• *For further information, contact:*

Cayman Island Department of Tourism
Box 67
Georgetown
Grand Cayman
BWI
TELEPHONE 809 949 0623

USA:
PO Box 90004
Atlanta, GA 30329
TELEPHONE 404 934 3959

UK:
Trevor House
100 Brompton Rd
London, SW3 IEX
TELEPHONE 071 581 9960

• *Additional reading:*

ROESSLER, C. (1989). *Diving and Snorkelling Guide to Grand Cayman Island*. Pisces Books.

COHEN, S. (1990). *Cayman Divers Guide*. Seapen Books.

Dominica

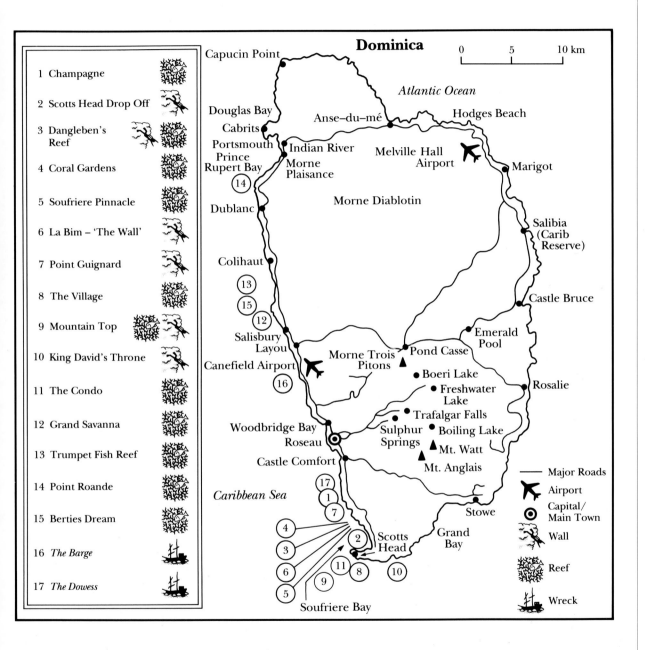

1	Champagne
2	Scotts Head Drop Off
3	Dangleben's Reef
4	Coral Gardens
5	Soufriere Pinnacle
6	La Bim – 'The Wall'
7	Point Guignard
8	The Village
9	Mountain Top
10	King David's Throne
11	The Condo
12	Grand Savanna
13	Trumpet Fish Reef
14	Point Roande
15	Berties Dream
16	*The Barge*
17	*The Dowess*

Dominica

0 5 10 km

Capucin Point

Atlantic Ocean

Douglas Bay
Cabrits
Anse–du–mé
Hodges Beach
Portsmouth
Prince
Rupert Bay
Indian River
Morne
Plaisance
Melville Hall Airport
Marigot
Dublanc
Morne Diablotin
Salibia (Carib Reserve)
Colihaut
Castle Bruce
Salisbury
Layou
Emerald Pool
Canefield Airport
Morne Trois Pitons
Pond Casse
Boeri Lake
Freshwater Lake
Rosalie
Woodbridge Bay
Roseau
Trafalgar Falls
Sulphur Springs
Boiling Lake
Castle Comfort
Mt. Watt
Mt. Anglais
Caribbean Sea
Stowe
Scotts Head
Grand Bay
Soufriere Bay

— Major Roads
✈ Airport
◉ Capital/ Main Town
Wall
Reef
Wreck

Dominica is known as 'The nature island of the Caribbean'. It is the least developed of the Windward and Leeward Islands, as it was the last stronghold for the Carib Indians. It is unlike any other island in the region!

The Carib presence, coupled with guerilla raids of escaped African slaves known as Maroons, and the difficult terrain hindered the development of large plantations. This fortunate lack of growth during the period of European colonization throughout the rest of the Caribbean islands has resulted in Dominica's unique status. Though it is among the largest of the Windward Islands, its population, at 82 000, is the smallest of the group.

While other islands have suffered severe reef damage from the development of beach front property, pollution of in-shore reefs and removal of mangrove swamps, Dominica has been saved from much of this fate. To well travelled scuba divers, the opening-up of a pristine destination is exciting. This is Dominica, only recently introduced to the diving world.

The underwater scenery of Dominica is as spectacular as that above with the rugged terrain continuing into the sea. Shallow reefs lead out to dramatic drop offs and sheer walls, most covered with tremendous black coral trees and huge barrel and tube sponges. The

volcanic action has formed arches and caves, now heavily encrusted with marine life. Not found on many other islands, there is also a marine sub-aquatic hot freshwater spring just offshore only 10 to 20 ft deep, known as **'Champagne'**. Fresh water bubbles drift slowly through holes and cracks in the rock formation towards the surface, appearing like liquid crystal glistening in the sunlight. This is the perfect ending to a night dive as one ascends from the nearby reef to the hot bubbles and experiences nature's sauna. On almost every night dive at 'Champagne', divers are greeted by schools of squid, enhancing the already exotic atmosphere.

As on any island, each shop has its favourite dive sites, depending on their location.

Among the most popular sites is **Scotts Head Drop Off**, a 20 ft ledge, with a dramatic drop-

'Champagne dive site' (Dominica)

Martha Watkins Gilkes surrounded by yellowtail snapper (ALICE BAGSHAW)

off to over 120 ft. The walls are covered in large tube sponges, gorgonia and occasional massive black coral trees, as large as a diver.

Dangleben's Reef, located between Point Guignard and Soufriere, is part of a reef system which runs perpendicular from the shore. The outer section is made up of pinnacles which range from 30 to 70 ft deep. The average depth is 50 ft, and, although the bottom drops much deeper, the recommended limit is 120 ft. One must also be aware of the presence of currents in the area. There is a rich coral growth and an abundance of reef fish such as snappers, margate, blackbar soldierfish and grunts.

The **Coral Gardens**, also between Soufriere and Point Guignard is actually part of Dengleben's Reef but does not feature the dramatic pinnacles. This is usually a calm, protected dive good for beginners, starting at 40 ft and sloping to 70 ft. Sea fans abound along with a wide variety of hard corals and small reef fish.

The **Soufriere Pinnacle** rises out of Soufriere Bay from around 150 ft to within 5 ft of the surface. The pinnacle is covered with soft and hard corals and a variety of tropical reef fish.

La Bim, 'The Wall', is an extensive 1½ mile wall which drops off from a 20 ft ledge to over 800 ft in some places. Large schools of blue and brown chromis mass among the pillar and boulder coral on the 20 ft ledge.

Point Guignard drops from 15 ft to 110 ft along the cliff face of the land. Several caves shelter large schools of blackbar soldierfish. One cave, opening at 45 ft, is large enough for a diver or two to enter, penetrating the rock wall about 40 ft. A mass of blackbar soldierfish part ranks as divers enter the opening. The roof is often inhabited by lobsters.

More advanced dives, on the Atlantic side of the island, include **King David's Throne**, **Mountain Top**, **The Village**, and **The Condo**. For all of them, wave action makes entry and exit usually difficult. However the visibility is generally excellent and the marine life pro-

Divers view cave filled with blackbar soldierfish (Scotts Head Pinnacle – Dominica)

Diver on wreck of the 'Dowess' (Dominica)

lific – occasional nurse sharks, snappers and pelagic fish, large schools of margate, massive sting rays frolicking on the nearby sand bottom and which are easily approached if the diver descends quietly.

The Condo is a large rock formation which offers a network of three intertwining caves, filled with soft corals, brightly coloured sponges, large schools of blackbar soldierfish and assorted reef fish that gently part as divers swim through. In fact, every crevice is filled with a mass of blackbar soldierfish.

Canefield tug (Dominica)

The Village, considered an experienced dive because of the high seas coming from the Atlantic waters, is a very exciting dive. At around 40 ft a granite shelf, running east to west, forms an overhang which is home to schooling fish and lobsters. A special feature is the sighting of schools of large margate and of black durgeons.

Without providing the sheer spectacular drop offs, the northern end of Dominica offers some magnificent diving. **Grand Savanna**, **Trumpet Fish Reef**, **Point Roande**, and **Berties Dream** are a few of the more popular sites. Some have permanent moorings installed to protect the coral reef from anchor damage.

Although wreck diving does not feature prominently on Dominica, a number of well known sites are worth visiting. One of these is **The Barge**, a shallow site in 40 ft, used mainly as a night dive because of the great number of star fish to be admired.

The latest wreck on Dominica is **The Dowess**, intentionally sunk as a diving site in July 1990 at Anse Bateau. Originally this 80 ft steel hull freighter plied the waters between the islands transporting produce. However, when she ran aground in Dominica waters the decision was taken to sink her. She now lies on a sloping sandy bottom in 50 to 73 ft of water, her stern section sitting end up.

When one looks at the pros and cons of diving in Dominica, a couple of negative points must be acknowledged. One of them is what is most beautifully called by the locals 'liquid sunshine', in other words the frequent – and often short – bursts of rainfall which may inconvenience the dedicated sun worshippers. During heavy rains too, the run-offs from the numerous rivers can cause near shore clouding. Another slight drawback on the leeward side of the island is the lack of large fish life, as the traditional fishing method, with wire fish pots, has taken its toll on the reef fish. Small fish are present however. The islanders are focusing their attention on this issue, in the hope of finding a solution to the problem. Finally the paucity of white sandy beaches, the absence of casinos, duty free shops and glittering night life may be to some a serious drawback.

For those, however, who want to immerse themselves in the island's lush mountain jungles – botanists, bird watchers, nature lovers, hikers and climbers, artists in search of dramatic views to paint or photograph – for the adventuresome scuba diver seeking unknown destinations, and for all those who simply want to explore one of the few very special places left on earth, then Dominica has much to offer.

It remains a land of untamed beauty, of wild and virtually unchanged mountains, of deep rain forests. The splendour of the **Emerald Pool**, a grotto fed by a waterfall lined with giant ferns, and of the **Trafalgar Waterfalls**, a double and sometimes triple fall, if there is enough rain, will no doubt capture the imagination of the traveller. The island is home of the sisserou, or imperial parrot, (Amazona Imperialis), a large, purple breasted parrot facing extinction. The endangered red-necked or Jaco parrot (Amazona Arausiaca) is also a Dominican native. Both are protected and Project Sisserou, which is now several years old, is giving them a fighting chance by providing additional land for their habitat. A hike to the parrot preserve or the rain forest is indeed highly recommended.

Although Dominica may lack jet airstrips, super highways, casinos, towering hotels, and be new to the diving world, the keen diver can be assured of a warm welcome and well qualified attention by the shops in existence on the island.

Dominica is 'the' island for the adventure diver who wants to explore the unexplored both under and above the water.

Directory

Dive Castaway
Box 5
Roseau, Dominica, WI
TELEPHONE 809 449 6244   FAX 809 449 6246

Dive Dominica
Box 63
Roseau, Dominica, WI
TELEPHONE 809 448 82118   FAX 809 448 6088

Dominica Dive Resort (Waitikubuli)
Box 34
Roseau, Dominica, WI
TELEPHONE 809 448 82638   FAX 809 448 85860

East Carib Dive, Ltd.
Box 483
Roseau, Dominica, WI
TELEPHONE 809 449 6575   FAX 809 449 66036

• *For further information, contact:*

Dominica Tourist Board
Box 73
Roseau, Dominica, WI
TELEPHONE 809 445 2351   FAX 809 448 58406

USA:
Caribbean Tourism Association
20 East 46th Street
New York, New York 10164
TELEPHONE 212 682 0435

UK:
Dominica Board of Tourism
1 Collingham Gardens
Earls Court
London SW5 OHW
TELEPHONE 071 373 8751   FAX 071 373 8743

Grenada and Carriacou

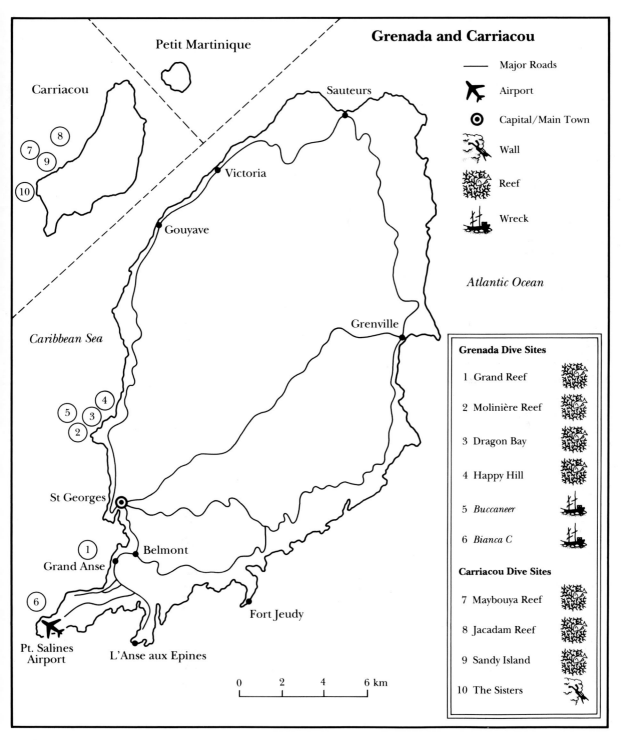

Petit Martinique

Carriacou

⑧
⑦
⑨
⑩

Sauteurs

Victoria

Gouyave

Grenville

Caribbean Sea

Atlantic Ocean

④
⑤ ③
②

St Georges

① Belmont
Grand Anse

⑥

Fort Jeudy

Pt. Salines
Airport

L'Anse aux Epines

0   2   4   6 km

Grenada and Carriacou

—— Major Roads

✈ Airport

◉ Capital/Main Town

Wall

Reef

Wreck

Grenada Dive Sites

1 Grand Reef

2 Molinière Reef

3 Dragon Bay

4 Happy Hill

5 *Buccaneer*

6 *Bianca C*

Carriacou Dive Sites

7 Maybouya Reef

8 Jacadam Reef

9 Sandy Island

10 The Sisters

Sailors claim they knew when they were approaching the island long before they could see the majestic mountains because of the smell of fresh spices in the air! Grenada is among the world's top suppliers of nutmeg and also grows a number of other spices. In fact, the island is referred to as 'The Spice Island'.

Grenada, the southernmost of the Windward Islands, 90 miles north of Trinidad, is a mountainous, lush and majestic island. Although it is only 21 by 12 miles, one can find in this small space beautiful white sand beaches, jungle covered mountains reaching up to 2 000 ft, numerous waterfalls and rivers.

Grenada's capital, **St Georges**, is the most picturesque harbour in the Caribbean, built around the crater of a volcano. Its colourful buildings, many dating back to the eighteenth century, are scattered up the hillsides among the flowering bougainvillaea, hibiscus and flamboyant. It is well worth visiting the town, wandering around the quaint shops, enjoying a fresh seafood meal in one of the local restaurants overlooking the harbour, and experiencing a water taxi ride in a local wooden rowing boat across the careenage.

Grenada is a three island state, with the smaller islands of Carriacou and Petit Martinique located in the group of islands known as the **Grenadines**. A few other island dependencies are under Grenada's rule; among them, Ile de Ronde, Kick-um-Jenny, Green Bird and Conference. All are uninhabited but extremely picturesque. The Grenadines are a chain of about 40 islands and islets, most only a dot on the yachting charts, with the majority belonging to Grenada's neighbour, St Vincent.

Petit Martinique, with only about 600 residents, is not tourist oriented and is virtually without any facilities for visitors. However, the 13 square mile **Carriacou**, 15 miles from Grenada, is well worth a visit for those who really want to get away from it all! Beautiful, secluded beaches abound and pristine, virginal reefs offer unexplored dive and snorkel locations. Carriacou is famous for its hand made wooden sailing boats traditionally considered to be the finest in the Caribbean. The christening and launching of a new boat always calls for a big 'jump up' (party) which can last for days. Most times, however, the island is a quiet sleepy Caribbean paradise – it is almost like stepping back into an age long gone on most other islands. Swimming, sailing, snorkelling, diving and just lazing around are the main activities of the day!

Diving is new to Grenada, and although there have been small operations over the years, only recently have several dive shops opened up on the island. Carriacou is following suit with a brand new dive shop.

All diving on Grenada is done on the protected leeward side where a variety of reefs, walls and wrecks are available to the diver. All diving is also done from boats as there are few reefs which can be reached from the beach.

Grand Reef, off Grand Anse Beach, starts in 20 ft of water and is a shelving reef where varied live coral such as plate coral, pillar coral and finger coral, provide shelter to a variety of colourful fish. Blue and brown chromis abound and green and black spotted

Crinoid

Orange file fish

moray can often be seen. A forest of soft gorgonia thrive in the shallow water near the anchorage. Masses of coral formations are separated by sand patches. The different levels of the reef give divers plenty of choice in diving depth.

Further up the leeward coast, a number of dive sites are located between Molinière and Halifax Bay. **Molinière Reef** starts in only 15 ft of water, gently sloping to around 100 ft, with a popular wreck site (see page 41) located at 80 ft. All dives start and end on the shallow reef, with the exploration of the wreck in between.

Dragon Bay also starts shallow but has a wall drop-off. As one descends, one can admire large 4–6 ft black coral trees over the wall.

Happy Hill and **Bucaner Bay** are nearby and offer similar shallow anchorage with sloping drop-offs and walls. There can be slight currents, and a drift dive across several of the bays is sometimes done, giving the diver the chance to explore various sites at once. On all these protected sites marine life abounds – blue and brown chromis, French angels, wrasses, parrotfish, schools of barracuda and more gentle fish such as spotted drums.

Wreck diving is a big attraction to many divers and Grenada will not disappoint them!

The **Buccaneer**, a 42 ft two-masted steel hull sloop, lies on her starboard side in Molinière Bay. She rests in 75 ft on a gentle slope. Although not a difficult dive, there can be current on the site. She was sunk around 1977 as a diving site. Covered in soft corals and hydroids, she offers superb photographic opportunities. In addition to the structure itself, the site provides the chance to observe a school of garden eels gently swaying in the sand and a yellow headed jaw fish is always nearby in his permanent burrow, popping up to nibble at a passing bit of plankton. Recently, there has

been a resident sea horse clinging to a nearby gorgonia. A nice ending to the dive is the exploration of the shallow Molinière Reef which ascends to 15 ft. Coral encrusted lava flows gently tumble down the sand slope, forming channels through which divers can swim.

The most famous wreck of Grenada, and among the largest to be dived in the Caribbean, is a 584 ft lady who will be always remembered throughout Grenada. A large bronze statue of Jesus Christ, entitled 'Christ of the Deep' stands in her honour and to her memory in the heart of St Georges. The **Bianca C** sank on 24 October 1961. This Italian cruise liner belonged to the Costa family and was carrying passengers on a Caribbean pleasure cruise. As she sat at anchor in the harbour, preparing to depart, on 22 October 1961, an explosion caused a fire that quickly spread. Two crew members were killed but no other lives were lost. The Grenadian people rushed to the rescue of the passengers in anything that would stay afloat, taking them ashore, into their homes and lives after the accident. As a result of their heroic efforts, the Costa family presented 'Christ of the Deep' statue, in memory of the warm hearted generosity of the Grenadian people.

After the fire, the *Bianca C* was towed out of harbour to prevent damage to other ships, by the British frigate HMS *Londonderry* who had joined in the rescue operation. She sank off Point Saline, on the southwest corner of the island, coming to rest on her starboard side in 160 ft of water. The port side is slightly higher sitting in 150 ft and the stern lies in 115 ft.

Covered in massive black coral trees, the site attracts pelagic marine life such as big groupers, jew fish, large barracuda, horse eye and black jacks. One can also observe more gentle life such as queen angelfish as well as a large pair of French angelfish which have taken up residence there.

French angelfish

Much still remains on the ship, although the propellers were salvaged. Sadly, in 1989, foreigners operating a dive shop (now closed) removed many remembrances of her grand days, including the bell, and much of the china and cutlery which could be seen by divers as they swam through the super-structure. However, the massive remaining structure is still an awesome sight.

The *Bianca C* is not a beginner's dive. Strong currents can make the descent and ascent difficult and the necessary decompression, while hanging on the anchor rope, especially challenging. Photographers, even very experienced ones, loaded with cumbersome equipment, must take great care, although the site does offer some spectacular photographic opportunities.

For experienced divers, especially those keen on wrecks, this is an exciting site. The best part of the ship to explore is from the smoke stack back to the stern section, as the open superstructure and tremendous amount of growth add to the thrill of this wonderful dive.

Today, the *Carla C*, an exact sister ship to the *Bianca C*, makes weekly calls on Grenada, bringing tourists to enjoy the spice island and providing an additional reminder of the *Bianca C*.

Nearby Carriacou also offers some spectacular diving sites, some of the most popular including the reefs around the islands of Maybouya and Jacadam, both uninhabited and a stone's throw from Carriacou itself. Unspoiled reefs can also be found around Sandy Island, although they are shallow and more suitable for snorkelling than scuba diving.

The **Sisters** is a dramatic wall dive, just off Carriacou, which drops to 300 ft.

There is only one dive shop on Carriacou, which claims, however, over 30 sites, including beach entries, wall and caves dives.

A live-aboard sailing boat dive operation out of Grenada enables small group of four to explore these pristine reefs.

The development of diving in Grenada and Carriacou is at a young stage and has suffered 'growing pains'. Over the past few years, several shops have opened, closed or changed hands. There is no recompression chamber, although there is an evacuation plan to nearby islands for treatment. However, this is not always well organized and evacuation is an expensive procedure. A dive accident insurance is thoroughly recommended!

Although all shops have boats, entry is from the beach, thus loading and off loading of heavy gear and delicate camera equipment can be difficult. Some shops offer help with carrying all gear.

Directory

Grenada

Starwind
Mosden Cumberbatch
Grenada Yacht Service
Box 183
St Georges
Grenada, West Indies
Telephone 809 440 2508/2883 (work)
   809 440 3678 (home)

Dive Grenada
David MacNaghten
Box 441
St Georges
Grenada, West Indies
Telephone 809 444 4371 ext 630 (work)
   809 440 5875 (home)
Fax 809 444 4800

Associated hotels:

Ramada Anse Beach
Box 441
St Georges
Grenada, West Indies
Telephone 809 444 4371   Fax 809 444 4800

Grenada Aquatics
c/o Cobaya Beach Resort
Box 336
St Georges
Grenada, West Indies
Telephone 809 444 4129

Carriacou

Silver Beach Diving
c/o Silver Beach Resort
Hillsborough
Carriacou
Grenada, West Indies
TELEPHONE 809 443 7337   FAX 809 443 7165

• *For further information, contact:*

Grenada Tourism Department
The Carenage
Box 293
St Georges
Grenada, West Indies
TELEPHONE 809 440 2278/2001

USA:
141 East 44th Street, Suite 701
New York, New York 10017
TELEPHONE 212 687 9554

UK:
Grenada High Commission
1 Collingham Gardens
London SW5 OHW
TELEPHONE 071 370 5164/5
FAX 071 370 7040

St Kitts and Nevis

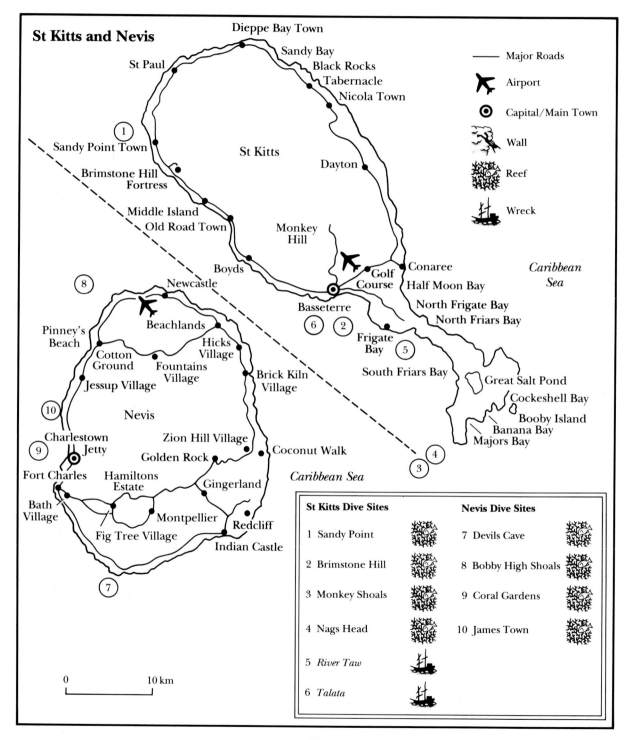

St Kitts and Nevis

Dieppe Bay Town
Sandy Bay
St Paul
Black Rocks
Tabernacle
Nicola Town

—— Major Roads

✈ Airport

◉ Capital/Main Town

Wall

Reef

Wreck

St Kitts

1

Sandy Point Town

Dayton

Brimstone Hill
Fortress

Middle Island
Old Road Town

Monkey
Hill

Boyds

Caribbean
Sea

8

Newcastle

Conaree

Golf
Course

Half Moon Bay

North Frigate Bay

North Friars Bay

Beachlands

Pinney's
Beach

Hicks
Village

Basseterre

6   2

Frigate
Bay

5

Cotton
Ground
Fountains
Village

Brick Kiln
Village

South Friars Bay

Jessup Village

10

Nevis

Great Salt Pond

Cockeshell Bay

Charlestown
Jetty

Zion Hill Village

Coconut Walk

Booby Island
Banana Bay
Majors Bay

9

Golden Rock

4

Fort Charles

Hamiltons
Estate

Gingerland

Caribbean Sea

3

Bath
Village

Fig Tree Village

Montpellier

Redcliff

Indian Castle

7

0   10 km

St Kitts Dive Sites		Nevis Dive Sites	
1 Sandy Point		7 Devils Cave	
2 Brimstone Hill		8 Bobby High Shoals	
3 Monkey Shoals		9 Coral Gardens	
4 Nags Head		10 James Town	
5 *River Taw*			
6 *Talata*			

St Kitts and Nevis, with only two dive operators on St Kitts and one on Nevis, are relatively unknown to divers. This, of course, means that they are both undamaged and unspoiled.

Two of the interesting sites on St Kitts are Sandy Point and Brimstone Hill.

Sandy Point is an extensive 50 ft reef that drops to 150 ft, although divers should not descend below 130 ft for safety. Strong currents that turn the dive into a drift, restrict this site to experienced divers only.

At **Brimstone Hill**, mini walls and high canyons are covered in coral growth and large barrel sponges. The site was used for anchorage when Brimstone Hill Fort, an old British fort, was at its peak and numerous old anchors can be seen.

Near Nevis, on the south side of St Kitts, Monkey Shoals and Nags Head Reef are found. **Monkey Shoals**, in the St Kitts – Nevis Passage, also known as the Narrows, is in 50 ft of water. A variety of hard coral formations are scattered across the bottom with sandy patches in between. The site has little or no current and is suitable for beginners, although there can be a surface swell.

Nags Head, also in the Narrows, starts in 30 ft and plunges to a sandy bottom at 80 ft. As the site is on the southernmost part of St Kitts, where the Atlantic and Caribbean meet, there can be strong currents and consequently a drop in visibility.

The *River Taw* and the *Talata* are two wrecks in the waters around St Kitts.

The ***River Taw***, a 148 ft freighter that used to ply the waters between St Kitts and Puerto Rico, rests in 45 ft off Frigate Bay where she sank around 1979, after running aground during a storm. She was successfully pulled off the rocks but went down at anchor because of the damage she had sustained. She now lies broken into two pieces. Her propeller and engine remain intact but most of the other features were salvaged. Divers can safely swim through the structure where yellowtail snapper are always in residence.

Efforts are also being made to establish an artificial reef near the wreck, out of discarded car bodies. Marine life is being quickly attracted and it is hoped that it will soon be thriving.

The 120 ft ***Talata*** lies off Basseterre, capital of St Kitts, in 60 ft of water and is sitting on a coral reef. She sank on her own around 1986 as she was in bad repair and had been neglected. The structure is broken up and penetration of what remains is not safe. As is true of any wreck site, marine life is attracted to the structure. Lobsters live inside and turtles are often spotted around the *Talata*. On this dive too, divers will experience something quite unique, as fresh, hot water bubbles out of a volcanic vein near the wreck.

Nevis sites include Devils Cave, Bobby High Shoals and the Coral Gardens.

Devils Cave, on the south side of Nevis is a thriving coral grotto in 40 ft of water. As divers swim through the coral formations, hardened lava flows can be seen running amidst the coral. There are several tunnels divers can penetrate. One of them starts in 40 ft of water, with a large 12 ft opening and spirals upward with the divers emerging through a 6 ft opening in only 8 ft of water where there is a massive anchor. Divers must swim in a single line as the tunnel is narrower towards the shallow end. Another interesting formation nearby is a coral arch with its base in 30 ft of water, leading to a large (15 ft) blow hole. Divers can swim through the arch, into this blow hole which leads into another smaller hole (approximately 10 ft wide). Although a low coral reef shelf separates the two, an experienced and careful diver could enter the second hole from the first. Both have large openings where divers can exit, emerging in

Diver with scorpion fish

about 10 ft of water. These holes are filled with blackbar soldierfish, juvenile yellowtail damsels, tiny schooling silvery, iridescent fish which part, flow and contour the divers as one swims through. Often eagle and sting rays are on the site as well as the usual French grunt and squirrelfish. Visibility is often over 100 ft, however the currents can make it drop to around 40 ft. In this case, it is suitable only for experienced divers. With good visibility, this site is an absolute underwater photographer's paradise.

Bobby High Shoals, in the Narrows, between Nevis and St Kitts, is only in 30 ft of water, but the presence of strong currents restrict it to experienced divers. The reef formation consists of ledges and overhangs with lobsters often tucked underneath.

Coral Gardens is a 50 ft reef that slopes gently to 70 ft. Ledges and overhangs are also a main feature here, where nurse sharks can be seen resting. Schools of Atlantic spade fish often swim nearby. Extremely large sea fans

Blackbar soldierfish

with flamingo tongue snails dining on them are another delightful sight for the divers.

Nevis has no known wreck, but one site causes great excitement to the archaeologically minded diver. It is **James Town**, the first settlement on the Western coast of Nevis. It is not explored on a regular basis, as often there is nothing to see, the shifting sand covering what little structure has been sighted in the past. It is generally accepted that James Town now lies below the sea, just off the west coast.

It is commonly thought, that the port town, literally, slipped into the sea as a result of a tidal wave or an earthquake. Some documents record this as happening on 30 April 1680, while others note 1860 as the year of the destruction. In his book *The Shipwrecks of the Western Hemisphere*, Robert Marx states that this dramatic event took place on 6 April 1690. He also mentions that in 1961, during an exploratory dive on the site he located a number of buildings protruding above the sea bed, in addition to 20 huge cannon.

Local fishermen and scuba divers claim, as has been told for decades, that the church bells can be heard tolling, when they are near the area. One diver confirmed that he had seen stone remains which could be the wall of an ancient building, however this has never been photographed nor documented. Marine salvage expert and treasure hunter, Teddy Tucker of Bermuda, has also said that, many years ago, he saw some remains of the town.

The curator of the Museum of Nevis, Joan Robinson, has done the most in-depth research on this subject and has found many contradictions to the generally accepted truth about James Town. The exact location is a mystery. Perhaps, one day, a lucky diver will chance upon some definite evidence which will help to clarify some of the mystery shrouding this ghost town.

St Kitts and Nevis are definitely for those who want to explore unknown destinations and are in search of exciting adventure.

Directory

St Kitts

Kenneth Dive Center
(Owner) Kenneth Samuel
Basseterre, St Kitts, West Indies
TELEPHONE 809 465 7043/2670
FAX 809 465 6472

Pro Divers
(Owner) Austin MacLeod
Box 65
Basseterre, St Kitts, West Indies
TELEPHONE 809 465 2754   FAX 809 465 1057

Nevis

Scuba Safaris
(Owner) Ellis Chaderton
Oualie Beach Club
Nevis, West Indies
TELEPHONE 809 469 9518   FAX 809 469 9619

• For further information, contact:

St Kitts and Nevis Tourist Board
Church Street, Box 132
Basseterre, St Kitts, West Indies
TELEPHONE 809 465 2629   FAX 809 465 8794

USA:
414 East 75th Street
New York, New York 10021
TELEPHONE 212 535 1234   FAX 212 897 4789

UK:
c/o Organisation of Eastern Caribbean States
Suite 437
High Holborn House
52 High Holborn
London, WC1V 6RB
TELEPHONE 071 242 3131

St Lucia

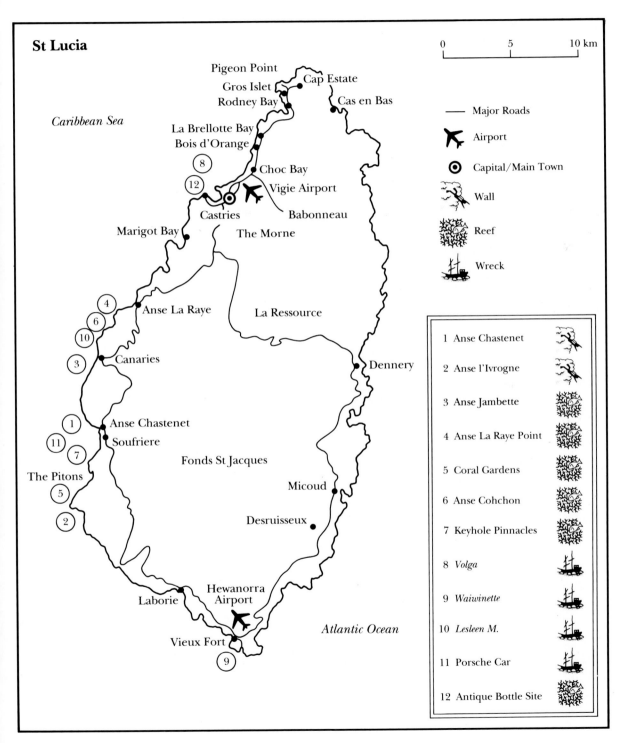

St Lucia

0   5   10 km

Pigeon Point
Cap Estate
Gros Islet
Cas en Bas
Rodney Bay

Caribbean Sea

La Brellotte Bay
Bois d'Orange

⑧

⑫

Choc Bay

Vigie Airport

Castries

Babonneau

Marigot Bay

The Morne

④

⑥

⑩

Anse La Raye

La Ressource

③

Canaries

Dennery

①

⑪

⑦

Anse Chastenet

Soufriere

Fonds St Jacques

The Pitons

⑤

Micoud

②

Desruisseux

Hewanorra
Airport

Laborie

Vieux Fort

Atlantic Ocean

⑨

— Major Roads

✈ Airport

⊙ Capital/Main Town

Wall

Reef

Wreck

1 Anse Chastenet

2 Anse l'Ivrogne

3 Anse Jambette

4 Anse La Raye Point

5 Coral Gardens

6 Anse Cohchon

7 Keyhole Pinnacles

8 *Volga*

9 *Waiwinette*

10 *Lesleen M.*

11 Porsche Car

12 Antique Bottle Site

St Lucia is a magical island to explore both on land and underwater. By many Caribbean islands' standards, the diving is virginal as the island has only recently become known to the international scuba diving world.

St Lucians have adopted towards diving a unique attitude in the Caribbean. While most islands are impatient to bring in and cash in on as many tourists as possible, without much thought given to conserving marine life, St Lucia has, from the very start, been innovative enough to realise the serious repercussions overdiving could have on her beautiful reefs. Thus, the Fisheries Department (responsible for scuba diving), through the Ministry of Agriculture, has begun efforts to safeguard the reef by controlling the number of diving businesses. Although nothing definite has been done towards this as yet, it is encouraging to see that those responsible are aware

Diver with a colourful sponge

and ready to take the necessary measures to protect this beautiful, yet fragile marine environment. The establishment of marine parks is one definite step which has already been taken to this end.

Nearly all of the diving sites offered by the various shops are on the calm leeward western side of the island (the Caribbean side).

As well as many exciting reefs abounding with colourful fish life, St Lucia offers one of the best beach entries in the Caribbean.

Directly off **Anse Chastenet**, an underwater shelf drops off from about 10 ft to over 150 ft. An amazingly dramatic wall! In the various depths they choose to explore – a choice made easy by the wall effect – divers will come across huge gorgonia, black coral trees, gigantic barrel sponges, tube sponges, encrusting sponges, over 25 species of coral, and a mass of reef life both invertebrate and fish. Small

Martha Watkins Gilkes with colourful sponge

octopus, coral banded shrimp, arrow crabs and schools of fish such as sergeant majors, grey and blue chromis, blue tang, French grunt and goatfish, all congregate there.

Other popular sites include **Anse l'Ivrogne**, **Anse Jambette**, **Anse La Raye Point**, the **Coral Gardens**, **Anse Cohchon** and the **Keyhole Pinnacles**. There is a myriad of other sites, with each diving operation having its favourite.

The Keyhole Pinnacles, four sea mounts formations, rise from the 75 ft bottom to within about 10 ft of the surface. They are covered in a variety of marine life such as gorgonia and sponges in vivid oranges and yellows.

St Lucia boasts also some interesting wrecks to dive. Just outside Castries is the *Volga*, easily accessible in only 20 ft of water. On the southern point of the island and in 90 ft of water, lies the *Waiwinette*, a large freighter. The depth and the currents around the site make it suitable only for the more experienced divers.

The best known and most popular wreck is that of the *Lesleen M.*, a 165 ft, 400 ton metal freighter which was sunk in June 1986 by the Fisheries Management Division to encourage fish life. Owned by the McQuilkins of St Lucia, she carried cargo between the islands and South America. She now lies in 65 ft of water, sitting upright on a sandy bottom, just south of the village of Anse la Raye. The top deck which is only 35 ft down can be seen from the surface. Soft corals and hydroid are beginning to cover her hull and small reef fish have taken up residence, with the odd large snapper visiting! The anchor winch, mast, lengths of chain and many of the port holes are still intact, so is the propeller which is covered in growth. With care, experienced divers can enter the engine room and hold. As there can be a current, especially on the surface, this is not an ideal dive for the novice. It is, however, an exciting wreck for the good diver with some experience and certainly for the underwater photographer.

In the middle of Anse Chastenet Bay, in 45 ft of water, lies a **Porsche car**, intentionally sunk to attract marine life and which previously belonged to the owner of the resort!

The wrecks which have been mentioned are all relatively new, although it is known that numerous ancient ones exist but their locations are not general knowledge. According to Robert Marx, seven large British ships went down on the leeward side of the island during the 1817 Hurricane. The locations of some are said to be known by local divers!

Finally, for those keen on hunting antique bottles, the entrance to **Castries** harbour can be a rich and rewarding site to dive, although there is limited reef life, the bottom being mostly sand.

Combining the beauty of its underwater world to the tropical ambience of the island itself, St Lucia constitutes a destination well worth pursuing.

Directory

Buddies Scuba
Vigie Marina
Castries, St Lucia
TELEPHONE 809 452 5288/7044

Dophin Divers
Rodney Bay Marina
Box 1538
Castries, St Lucia
TELEPHONE 809 452 9922   FAX 809 452 8524

Scuba St Lucia
Anse Chastenet Hotel
Box 7000
Soufriere, St Lucia
TELEPHONE 809 459 7000   FAX 809 459 7700

Windjammer Diving
Windjammer Landing, Villa Beach
Box 1504
Castries, St Lucia
TELEPHONE 809 452 1311   FAX 809 452 0907

• *For further information, contact:*

St Lucia Tourist Board
Location: Pointe Seraphine
Box 221
Castries, St Lucia
TELEPHONE 809 452 4094

USA:
9th Floor
820 2nd Avenue
New York, New York 10017
TELEPHONE 212 867 1950   FAX 212 370 7867

UK:
c/o Organization of Eastern Caribbean States
Suite 437
High Holborn House
52 High Holborn
London WC1V 6RB
TELEPHONE 071 242 3131

Turks and Caicos

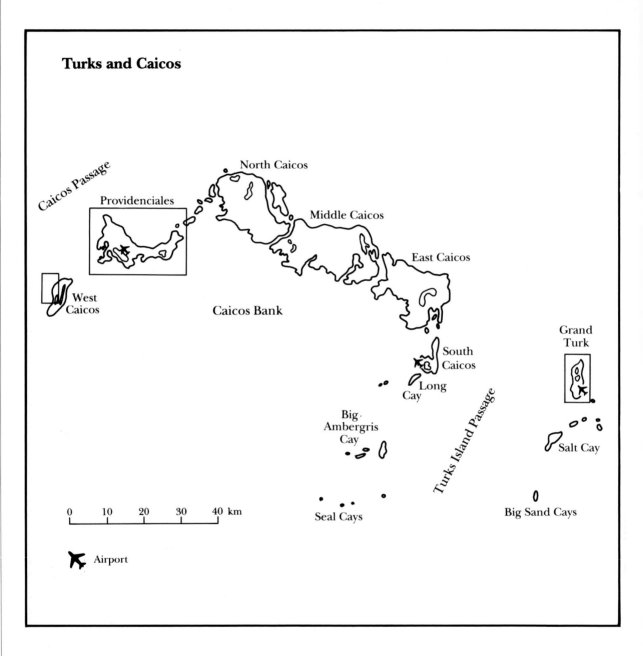

Turks and Caicos

Caicos Passage

North Caicos

Providenciales

Middle Caicos

East Caicos

West Caicos

Caicos Bank

Grand Turk

South Caicos

Long Cay

Big Ambergris Cay

Turks Island Passage

Salt Cay

Seal Cays

Big Sand Cays

0   10   20   30   40 km

Airport

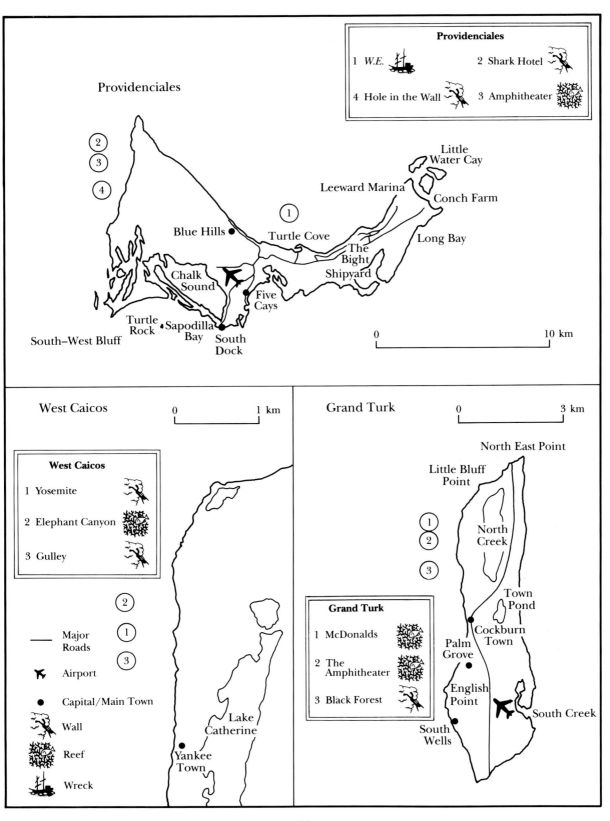

Providenciales

Providenciales

1 *W.E.*
2 Shark Hotel
4 Hole in the Wall
3 Amphitheater

2
3
4

Blue Hills •

Turtle Cove

1

Leeward Marina

Little
Water Cay

Conch Farm

Long Bay

The
Bight
Shipyard

Chalk
Sound

Five
Cays

Turtle
Rock • Sapodilla
Bay

South
Dock

South–West Bluff

0   10 km

West Caicos

0   1 km

West Caicos

1 Yosemite

2 Elephant Canyon

3 Gulley

2

1

3

Major
Roads

Airport

Capital/Main Town

Wall

Reef

Wreck

Lake
Catherine

Yankee
Town

Grand Turk

0   3 km

North East Point

Little Bluff
Point

1
2

North
Creek

3

Town
Pond

Cockburn
Town

Palm
Grove

Grand Turk

1 McDonalds

2 The
    Amphitheater

3 Black Forest

English
Point

South Creek

South
Wells

The Turks and Caicos are a chain of islands divided into two groups: Turks and Caicos. The marine life surrounding them is rivalled by few other Caribbean islands. To the tremendous variety in diving sites – from shallow reefs to dramatic walls – the islands also boast their own resident pet dolphin, Jojo, who lives completely free. Jojo, a wild Atlantic bottle nose dolphin, has been made a national treasure of the Turks and Caicos, yet interacts of his own free will, on a regular (usually daily) basis with divers, snorkellers, boaters and swimmers, especially around the island of Providenciales.

The mainstay for the islands is tourism and selling their natural resources – sea, sun and sand. The islanders caught on early to the need to protect what they rely on for daily subsistence. Having made conservation their top priority, they are not allowing spear fishing nor the taking of marine life while scuba diving. Thus, it is not surprising that the Turks and Caicos are also home for two interesting conservation-slanted projects. Located on Providenciales, the Protection of Reefs and Islands from Degradation and Exploitation (PRIDE) is based at the island Sea Center, a commercial conch farm. This 16-year-old US based foundation has helped guide the conservation of the islands in various worthwhile projects. At the **Sea Center**, an interesting tour can be made to view the life cycle and development of the conch. A number of the conch that hatch are released back into the wild, while the rest are marketed for their delicious meat and beautiful shell.

Into The Blue is also based on Providenciales. This is a dolphin rehabilitation project which, at the time of writing, has taken three captive dolphins. They have been taught how to survive in the wild and have been freed. Plans to continue with this dolphin rehabilitation are under way.

The islands also cater for the safety of their divers by providing a recompression chamber on Providenciales.

Around all the islands, there are wrecks and reefs to explore. One of the most interesting wrecks lies on the north side of Providenciales. The **W.E.**, a 185 ft ship, was sunk in July 1987 as a diving site. Being in 100 ft of water, she is for advanced divers only. The **W.E.** was an inter-island freighter, that missed a cut into the deep water and ran aground. For three years, she sat on sandy beach until she was purchased by a water sports group who sought the government's permission to sink her at her present location. Jew fish, green moray eels and nurse sharks are among the marine life often seen around the wreck, although growth is somewhat limited due to her young age and depth.

The Northwest point of Providenciales, within the Princess Alexandra National Marine Park, has a number of popular reef sites including Shark Hotel, Amphitheater and Hole in the Wall.

Shark Hotel is a mini-wall which starts around 45 ft and drops steeply to 110 ft. A further drop to 130 ft exposes coral overhangs, crevices and ravines. Near the surface of the wall are several giant pillar corals, one larger than a man! The marine life is varied with pelagic fish such as eagle rays often coming in from the deeper water.

The **Amphitheater**, also called **Shy Elephant**, in about 90 ft, is formed by a large coral ledge. A large elephant ear sponge (thus the name), measuring about 8 ft, a large barrel sponge and a wealth of black coral make this reef particularly attractive. However, it seems that the 'Shy Elephant Sponge' is in trouble as a disease is attacking ear sponges in the area. Hopefully, this will not cause irreparable damage. Horse eye jack are always in residence.

Hole in the Wall starts at around 40 ft and drops to a maximum depth of 140 ft. Its main interest lies in the presence of large brain coral colonies at about 70 ft where the wall

Martha Watkins Gilkes with orange elephant ear sponge (ALICE BAGSHAW)

becomes very sheer and plunges to 140 ft. Numerous deep crevices and cuts and a delicate chimney formation are covered with growth. Delicate tunicates abound and large West Indian spider crabs hide in some of the crevices.

Grand Turk is fringed on its west coast by a beautiful six mile reef which is only a ¼ mile from the shore. Over two dozen named sites of various depths are to be explored along this reef.

A favourite location bears the curious name of **McDonalds**! This 70 ft site provides a magnificent coral arch which divers can swim through. Loggerhead and green turtles are often spotted as are bottle nose dolphins, in the midst of a rich and varied marine life.

The **Amphitheater** on the northwest side of Grand Turk is permanently moored to protect the coral formations. This horseshoe-shaped reef lies in 40 ft of water and is home for a large colony of graceful eels who reside on the white sandy bottom. Divers often have the pleasure of spotting dolphins and rays (sting rays, manta and eagle rays) in the area.

The **Black Forest** takes its name from the dramatic black coral covering the wall. The dive can be made as a boat or beach entry as it is near the beach of Guanahani Beach Hotel. The wall starts in 35 ft of water and drops to a ledge in 220 ft, continuing to the abyss!

Uninhabited **West Caicos**, located south west of Providenciales, offers some spectacu-

Diver with turtle

lar diving and should not be left out. Three especially good sites are **Yosemite**, **Gulley** and **Elephant Canyon**. **Yosemite** is an exceptionally beautiful wall dive. Four massive coral outcroppings project from around 50 ft, sloping to 130 ft and then dramatically plunging sharply to around 250 ft.

Gulley is a deep narrow gully which allows the diver to swim through the cut lined with several large barrel sponges. One unique feature, if one happens to be lucky and diving around mid-August, are the banana sponges. According to Captain Bob Gascoine, author of an extensive dive guide to the Turks and Caicos, 'once a year, around this time, they make love. The male releases a cloud of sperm followed by the females releasing an orange stringy mess of eggs'.

Elephant Canyon is home to the largest known sponge in the Turks and Caicos. This giant orange elephant ear sponge measures over 10 ft and is almost perfectly round. However, because of the disease that is, at the time of writing, affecting this type of sponge, giving them a 'swiss cheese' appearance, there is concern over this majestic specimen. It is strategically located at the end of a sand chute and veils a small cave filled with groupers and margate. A large variety of other types of hard coral grow in the vicinity and visibility is usually at least 100 to 200 ft.

For the serious diver, the Turks and Caicos are certainly among the top diving locations in the Caribbean. Fortunately, the careful conservation of the marine environment will ensure that it remains so.

Diver with peacock flounder

Directory

Please note that the following is not necessarily an exhaustive list of all dive operators on the islands but a cross-section.

Grand Turk

Blue Water Divers
Location: Salt Raker Inn
Box 124
Grand Turk, Turks and Caicos, BWI
TELEPHONE 809 946 2260   FAX 809 946 2432

Off the Wall Diving and Watersports
Box 177
Grand Turk, Turks and Caicos, BWI
TELEPHONE 809 946 2159

Omega Divers
TELEPHONE 809 946 22332

Providenciales

Dive Provo
Ramada Turquoise Reef Resort
Providenciales, Turks and Caicos, BWI
TELEPHONE 809 946 5029   FAX 809 946 5936

Erebus Inn
Box 238
Turtle Cove
Providenciales, Turks and Caicos, BWI
TELEPHONE 809 946 4240   FAX 809 946 4704

Flamingo Divers
Box 322
Turtle Cove Landing
Providenciales, Turks and Caicos, BWI
TELEPHONE 809 946 4193   FAX 809 946 4193

Provo Turtle Divers
Turtle Cove Marina
Providenciales, Turks and Caicos, BWI
TELEPHONE 809 946 4232   FAX 809 946 4326

Live aboard dive boats:

Aggressor
PO Drawer K
Morgan City, LA 70881- 000K USA
TELEPHONE 504 385 2416   FAX 504 384 0817
800 348 2628

Aquanaut
Box 113
Providenciales, Turks and Caicos, BWI
TELEPHONE 809 946 2160   FAX 809 946 4048

Sea Dancer
Location: Caicos Marine and Shipyard
1390 South Dixie Highway,
Suite 2213
Coral Gables, FL 33146
TELEPHONE 305 669 9391 or 800 9-Dancer
FAX 305 669 947

• For further information, contact:

Ministry of Tourism and Development
Grand Turk
Turks and Caicos, BWI
TELEPHONE 809 946 1300/1306

USA:
Franklin International Plaza
155 Alhambra Circle, Suite 312
Coral Gables, FL 33134
TELEPHONE 305 667 0966

UK:
3 Epirus Road
Fulham, London SW6 7UJ
TELEPHONE 071 376 2981   FAX 071 938 4793

• Additional references:

GASCOINE, B.(Capt). *Divers, Snorkellers and Visitors Guide to the Turks and Caicos.* Palm Publications, Box 113, Providenciales, Turks and Caicos Islands, BWI.

The US Virgin Islands

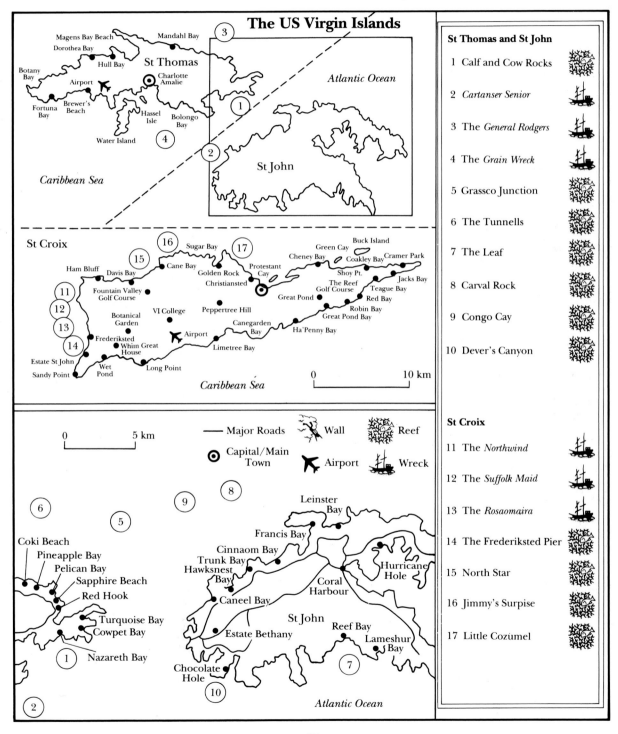

The US Virgin Islands

St Thomas

Magens Bay Beach
Dorothea Bay
Mandahl Bay
Hull Bay
St Thomas
Botany Bay
Airport
Charlotte Amalie
Brewer's Beach
Fortuna Bay
Hassel Isle
Bolongo Bay
Water Island

Atlantic Ocean

Caribbean Sea

St John

St Croix

Sugar Bay
Buck Island
Green Cay
Cheney Bay
Coakley Bay
Cramer Park
Ham Bluff
Davis Bay
Cane Bay
Golden Rock
Protestant Cay
Shoy Pt.
Jacks Bay
Fountain Valley Golf Course
Christiansted
The Reef Golf Course
Teague Bay
VI College
Peppertree Hill
Great Pond
Red Bay
Botanical Garden
Robin Bay
Canegarden Bay
Great Pond Bay
Frederiksted
Airport
Ha'Penny Bay
Whim Great House
Estate St John
Limetree Bay
Wet Pond
Long Point
Sandy Point

Caribbean Sea

0   10 km

— Major Roads
⊙ Capital/Main Town
✈ Airport
Wall
Reef
Wreck

0   5 km

Coki Beach
Pineapple Bay
Pelican Bay
Sapphire Beach
Red Hook
Turquoise Bay
Cowpet Bay
Nazareth Bay

Leinster Bay
Francis Bay
Cinnaom Bay
Trunk Bay
Hawksnest Bay
Hurricane Hole
Coral Harbour
Caneel Bay
St John
Estate Bethany
Reef Bay
Lameshur Bay
Chocolate Hole

Atlantic Ocean

St Thomas and St John

1 Calf and Cow Rocks
2 *Cartanser Senior*
3 The *General Rodgers*
4 The *Grain Wreck*
5 Grassco Junction
6 The Tunnells
7 The Leaf
8 Carval Rock
9 Congo Cay
10 Dever's Canyon

St Croix

11 The *Northwind*
12 The *Suffolk Maid*
13 The *Rosaomaira*
14 The Frederiksted Pier
15 North Star
16 Jimmy's Surpise
17 Little Cozumel

The US Virgin Islands are more developed both for diving and in general than most other Caribbean islands. Although they consist of over 50 cays and islets, three of them are well known and contain almost all of the population. St Thomas is the best known one, followed by St Croix which is the largest and constitutes the easternmost point of the USA, and then St John. Diving has developed alongside other tourist facilities and there are now 20 diving operations between the three islands. A local unspoken rule sets that the first boat on a dive site will be the only one and other boats will choose a different location, thus avoiding the overloading of a site with too many divers.

As these islands are American possessions, the dive boats are US Coast Guard inspected and must meet all the safety requirements, resulting in a higher standard than is usually found on other Caribbean islands. This is further enhanced by a good medical system and the presence of a recompression chamber facility on St Thomas. Although the weather is as one would expect on a tropical island, a northerly ground swell, during the winter months, can make some sites unsuitable for diving. However, this is not a major problem as there is a very large selection of sites to choose from.

St Thomas

Calf and Cow Rocks on the southeast end of St Thomas are so named as they have been mistaken for a migrating cow and calf humpback whale! The rocks project slightly above the water. Underwater archways, overhangs and a tunnel offer interesting photographic opportunities and exploration among schools of silverside fish, glassy sweepers and horse-eye jacks. The **Champagne Cork**, a tunnel in only 10 feet of water is of particular interest to divers who can swim through it in calm weather. In rough seas, the swells channel through the tunnel, spouting out of an overhead opening, thus the name! Nurse sharks often are found resting under the ledges. For the inexperienced diver, the surge near the surface of the rocks can cause some difficulty, so, in rough conditions, the site is recommended for the experienced diver only.

St Thomas boasts several popular wreck sites, including the **Cartanser Senior**, the **General Rodgers** and the **Grain Wreck**. The *Barges* is sometimes mentioned among them, but is much inferior to the other sites and does not merit being expanded upon.

The **Cartanser Senior**, a 190 feet steel hulled freighter which went down in 1979, constitutes an easy dive, suitable for beginners. She is located just off the east end of Buck Island and sits in only 35 feet of water. She originally transported goods during World War Two and rumour has it that she was then used for smuggling around the islands, until she was abandoned, sinking in Gregerie Channel in St Thomas. Being a navigational hazard, she was to be destroyed by the Corps of Engineers, but after intervention by the diving operators, she was moved just off Buck Island to 70 feet of water. Hurricane Alan then pushed her into shallow water where she now rests, broken into several pieces. Penetration into the wreck is easy and safe as the holds are open, allowing easy access to the engine room, cargo areas and other parts of the interior.

Due to the ease of the dive and the interest presented by the site, there are four permanent moorings to meet the daily demand of divers.

The **General Rodgers**, a 130 ft Coast Guard cutter, is dived both by the St Thomas and St John operators, due to the location. She was sunk in 1972 as a diving site off Pillsbury Sound and sits upright in 65 ft of water, with her deck at only 45 ft, making it an ideal wreck dive. The visibility is usually 60 to 68 ft. The propeller was left intact and is now covered in

Tubastrea polyps expand at night

Wreck of the 'General Rodgers' (St Thomas)

growth. Inside the forward hold, a spare propeller makes for a superb photo opportunity as do the hull and decks adorned with colourful orange tubastreas, sponges and invertebrate life. A large barracuda is often in residence, along with several grey angelfish.

The **Grain Wreck** was sunk on the south of St Thomas by the US Navy in 1992 and is located in 110 ft of water. Due to the depth, the entire wreck cannot be explored in one single dive.

Additional diving sites offered by the St Thomas operators are mentioned under St John dive sites.

St Croix

St Croix claims too her wreck sites. In Butlers Bay, on the West Coast of St Croix, three wrecks are lying close together, all intentionally sunk as diving sites: The **Northwind**, the **Suffolk Maid** and the **Rosaomaira**.

The 75 ft **Northwind**, lies in 45 ft of water; it was used as a set for a TV movie about the treasure hunter Mel Fisher, and after being abandoned was sunk in 1986.

The 140 ft **Suffolk Maid** met her final destiny after a hurricane damaged her in 1984. She now lies in 65 ft of water.

Octopus

The steel hulled freighter *Rosaomaira*, the largest of the three at 177 ft, rests on a slope with the wheelhouse at about 75 ft and the deepest part at 110 ft, thus being more suitable for the experienced diver. After capsizing in port, she was towed to her final resting place in April 1986.

The **Frederiksted Pier**, a 450 yard commercial pier off Frederiksted, is well known as a special dive in the day and even more so at night, which should not be missed. Situated in only 30 ft of water, it is an easy dive, although the entry and exit might present a few problems to the novice, as it can only be done either directly off the pier or by way of a steel ladder. It boasts a very rich and colourful marine life, such as sea horses which have made it their home and which are easier to locate at night. There is also a host of invertebrate marine life which should delight the keen photographer. The pilings are totally encrusted with sponges, and are alive with creatures such as arrow crabs, christmas tree worms, feather duster worms, brittle star fish and octopus, to name but a few. At the time of writing, there are plans to relocate the pier which causes concern over damaging the marine life existing there. However, some dive operators feel that much of it will get reestablished on the new location.

Other sites on St Croix worth mentioning include North Star, Jimmy's Surprise and Little Cozumel.

North Star is accessible from a boat or the beach, if the swell is not too big. At 35 ft a vertical wall starts which drops to 60 ft where an encrusted Danish anchor can be found lying on a sand plateau against the coral reef. Nearby, an overhang provides a home for silverside. The reef then drops again with 130 ft being the recommended limit for the dive. Large sea fans and bright orange elephant ear sponges cover the wall. Large creatures, such as an occasional manta or shark, are often spotted.

Jimmy's Surprise, west of Christiansted, is a pinnacle rising from the sea bed at 90 ft to 60 ft. A permanent mooring buoy marks the site. There can be currents around the pinnacle. An abundance of sea life can be found, including a variety of hard and soft corals, sea fans, schools of horse eye jacks, black tips and nurse sharks. More gentle marine creatures like queen angelfish are frequently spotted.

Little Cozumel, also on the western side of Christiansted, is reputed for its undercut ledge which drops from 50 to 60 ft. Goatfish, angelfish, barracuda and filefish can all be seen on this dive.

St John

St John, although the smallest of the US Virgins, is a very special island, as two thirds of it is left as a national park. Some of the most popular sites on St John (some of them are also covered by the St Thomas operators) include Grassco Junction, Tunnells, The Leaf, Carval Rock and Congo Cay.

Grassco Junction on the south west end of Grassy Cay is for the experienced diver, as it goes down to 80 ft. Several exceptional coral heads stand 20 ft high and larger marine life such as rays and turtles can be spotted.

The Tunnells, also called **The Arches and Tunnells**, situated on the west end of Thatch Cay at a depth of 40 ft, are formed by massive boulders resting against each other, thus forming passages, tunnels and rooms through which the divers can swim. There are at least six arches and two exceptionally long tunnels (60 ft) which are often filled with silverside fish. Glassy sweepers as well as soft corals grow on the rock faces of these passages ways.

The Leaf, off Reef Bay, slopes from 45 to 80 ft and is home for nurse sharks, rays and turtles.

Horse eye jacks

Carval Rock and **Congo Cay** are large rocks which rise above the water on the northwest between St John and St Thomas. The diver can descend to 90 ft and admire the rocks covered in sponges and gorgonian.

For a night dive, **Dever's Canyon**, sloping from 10 to 45 ft is a favourite site. Unusual orange balls anemones adorn the site and, on nearly every dive, a resident, massive, 500 lb green turtle can be seen sleeping under a ledge. Divers are not allowed to disturb or touch the turtle.

Most of the operators on St Thomas and St John dive the famous wreck of the ***Rhone***, in the British Virgin Islands, which is only a short boat trip across (a passport is required for entry unless one is a British citizen. For non US citizens a US tourist visa may be required to return to US waters). See British Virgin Islands chapter.

Considering the amount of diving activity in the US Virgin Islands, only a selection of sites and operators can be given in this guide. Refer to the directory for detail of sources.

Diver with grouper

Directory

As there are over 30 operators in the US Virgin Islands, a cross-section of some of them is given here.

St Thomas

Aqua Action Center
Red Hook, Box 15
St Thomas, USVI 00802
TELEPHONE 809 775 6285   FAX 775 1501

Caribbean Divers
56 Frydenhoj
St Thomas, USVI 00802
TELEPHONE 809 775 6384

Chris Sawyer Diving Center
41-6-1 Estate Frydenhoj
St Thomas, USVI 00802
TELEPHONE 809 775 7320   FAX 775 3757

Dive In
Box 5664
St Thomas, USVI 00803
TELEPHONE 809 775 6100   FAX 775 4024

Hi Tec Watersports
Box 1493
St Thomas, USVI 00804
TELEPHONE 809 774 5650

Joe Vogel Diving Co Inc
Box 7322
St Thomas, USVI 00801
TELEPHONE 809 775 7610   FAX 775 5144

St Thomas Diving Club
Box 7377
St Thomas, USVI 00801
TELEPHONE 809 776 2381

Underwater Safaris
Box 8469
St Thomas, USVI 00801
TELEPHONE 809 774 1350

VI Diving Schools
Box 9707
St Thomas, USVI 00801
TELEPHONE 809 774 8687   FAX 774 7368

St Croix

Anchor Dive Center
Box 5588
Christiansted
St Croix USVI 00823
TELEPHONE 809 778 1522   FAX 809 772 3059

Blue Dolphin Divers
Box 5261
Sunny Island
St Croix USVI 00840
TELEPHONE/FAX 809 773 8634

Cruzan Divers Inc
12 Strand St.
Fredericksted
St Croix USVI 00840
TELEPHONE 809 772 3701

Dive St Croix
59 King's Wharf
Box 3045
Christiansted, St Croix USVI 00840
TELEPHONE 809 773 2285

St John

Coral Bay Watersports
10-19 Estate Carolina
Coral Bay, St John USVI 00830
TELEPHONE/FAX 809 776 6850

Cruz Bay Watersports Co
Box 252
St John USVI 00831
TELEPHONE 809 776 6234   FAX 776 8303

Low Key Watersports
Box 431, Cruz Bay
St John USVI 00831
TELEPHONE 809 776 7048   FAX 776 7042

Paradise Watersports
Box 54, Cruz Bay
St John USVI 00831
TELEPHONE 809 776 6111   FAX 809 776 2030

St Johns Watersports
Box 70, Cruz Bay
St John USVI 00830
TELEPHONE 809 776 6256   FAX 809 776 7406

• For further information, contact:

US Virgin Islands Division of Tourism:
Box 6400
Charlotte Amalie
St Thomas, USVI 00804

USA:
US Virgin Islands Division of Tourism
1279 Avenue of the Americas
New York, New York 10020

UK:
US Virgin Islands Division of Tourism
2 Cinnamon Row, Plantation Wharf, York Place
London SW11 3TW

• Additional reading:

BOWER, S. and NYDEN, B. (1990). *Diving and Snorkelling Guide to The Virgin Islands*. Pisces Books.

St Vincent and the Grenadines

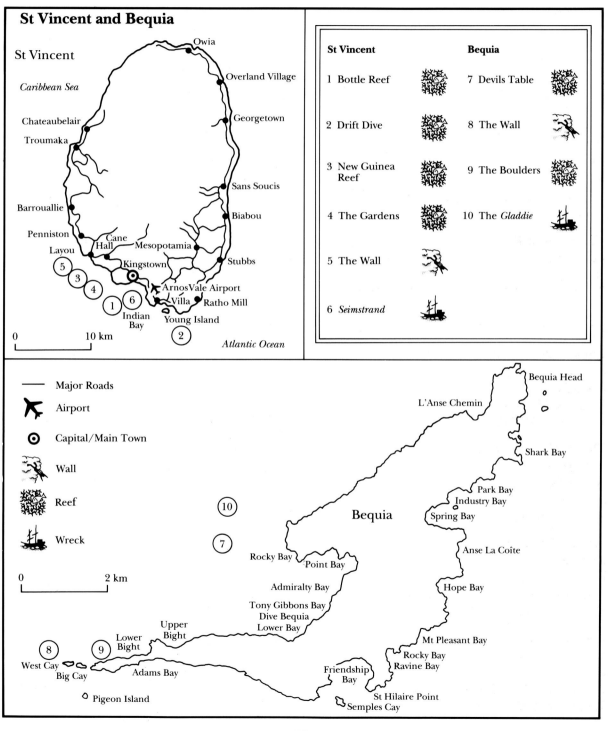

St Vincent and Bequia

St Vincent

Caribbean Sea

Owia
Overland Village
Georgetown
Chateaubelair
Troumaka
Sans Soucis
Barrouallie
Biabou
Penniston
Cane Hall
Mesopotamia
Layou
Kingstown
Stubbs
ArnosVale Airport
Villa
Ratho Mill
Indian Bay
Young Island

0   10 km

Atlantic Ocean

St Vincent	Bequia
1 Bottle Reef	7 Devils Table
2 Drift Dive	8 The Wall
3 New Guinea Reef	9 The Boulders
4 The Gardens	10 The *Gladdie*
5 The Wall	
6 *Seimstrand*	

— Major Roads
✈ Airport
⊙ Capital/Main Town
Wall
Reef
Wreck

0   2 km

Bequia

Bequia Head
L'Anse Chemin
Shark Bay
Park Bay
Industry Bay
Spring Bay
Anse La Côite
Rocky Bay
Point Bay
Admiralty Bay
Hope Bay
Tony Gibbons Bay
Dive Bequia
Lower Bay
Upper Bight
Lower Bight
Mt Pleasant Bay
Rocky Bay
Ravine Bay
West Cay
Friendship Bay
Big Cay
Adams Bay
St Hilaire Point
Semples Cay
Pigeon Island

Although they have much to offer to the discerning diver, St Vincent and the Grenadines Islands are still undiscovered and totally unspoilt.

Being a volcanic island, St Vincent has granite based sand which is heavier than coral sand and settles more quickly after any sea disturbance. This, generally, means better visibility. When diving in the waters around St Vincent, one can actually see the lava flows that once tumbled down the mountains into the sea. There are often deep ravines between the flows, forming mini-walls, covered in gorgonia and colourful sponges, with tropical fish among the marine growth.

There is a unique set-up for divers in St Vincent and the Grenadines. The various dive shops on St Vincent, Bequia, Canouan and Union have developed a cooperative system allowing divers to purchase a 10-dive package which enables them to dive in the various islands and to complete certification as well.

Some of the favourite sites, covered by Dive St Vincent which is owned and operated by Bill Tewes, include New Guinea Reef, Bottle Reef, The Garden, The Wall and the Drift Dive.

Bottle Reef, situated in the Kingstown harbour, begins as a gentle slope with a small wall starting at 25 ft and dropping to 91 ft and adorned with gorgonia, sea fans, sponges and black coral. Solitary Spanish mackerel glide by. During tarpon season (February to June) these sleek silver giants enhance the site. An added treat is the chance of finding an antique bottle. Fort Charlotte, a British fort built between 1796 and 1806, is perched above the site and it is thought that the array of bottles lying about arise from being tossed over from the fort. If there is a strong current, the site is limited to advanced divers.

The **Drift Dive**, located at Nanton Point, is only for advanced divers as there can be very heavy currents. The site, ranging from 25 to 88 ft has no coral and one operator describes it as a moonscape with large boulders scattered about. The main attraction is the astonishing fish population, not the site itself. As the diver drifts with the current, schools of reef fish abound, along with large groupers, snappers, spade fish and barracuda. A variety of moray eels (spotted, golden tail, vipers and some large green and occasionally a purple mouth) are to be admired too. This can be an exhilarating dive in the midst of large marine life, as the boat follows the drifting divers!

New Guinea Reef and **The Gardens** are so spectacular that often visiting divers request to repeat them. Both are suitable for all levels of divers.

New Guinea Reef offers all three species of the rare black coral. It drops from 25 ft to 105 ft, and during their descent, divers are immersed in the myriad of colours of numerous soft and hard corals and a variety of sponges. As the site has a permanent mooring, no damage is done to the surrounding corals by dropping an anchor. At 85 ft, a dramatic deep overhang descends to 100 ft. Divers can swim under the overhang, penetrating the coral about 40 ft. Trees of black coral interspersed with yellow sponges grace the wall. A large queen angelfish makes her home here, adding to the majestic beauty of this breathtaking underwater seascape.

Not far from the overhang, in another coral formation, a gold chain moray shares her residence with a black spotted moray, a very unusual arrangement! Pelagic fish seen at the site include black jack, Spanish mackerels, and bonito. Blue lace shrimp, coral banded shrimp, arrow crab, the occasional sea horses and the uncommon frog fish will enchant the photographer.

A colony of graceful garden eels, who make their permanent home in burrows in the sand near the descent line attached to the permanent mooring enhance further the sheer delight of this dive.

Diver explores the wreck of the 'Seimstrand' (St Vincent)

The Gardens slopes from 25 to about 120 ft and is usually done as the second dive of the day. For decompression safety reasons, the dives are limited to about 80 ft. The site is literally a carpet of finger coral where divers will discover a wealth of marine creatures such as extremely large, 18 inch, king crabs and, occasionally, yellow and orange frog fish. The top of the reef is home to large schools of French grunt and squirrelfish. More unusual, is the rare cherubfish, the world's smallest angel fish according to some experts, at only 1½ inch! This tiny beauty, not commonly seen, with its electric blue body and bright orange face is always on the site, often in pairs.

The Wall is a sheer drop from 30 to 112 ft, a 'free fall dive', as one operator describes it. There is a second small wall that drops down to 130 ft. Black coral, lobsters tucked in nooks and crannies, schools of snappers and other reef fish, are among the pleasures of this site. Occasionally, frog fish can be found there too. In the shallower depths, the diver will enjoy the magnificent sight of the juvenile yellowtail damselfish, whose body is covered in iridescent blue spots glowing like miniature lights.

Azure vase sponge

Wreck diving is available in St Vincent. According to Robert Marx, in his book *The Shipwrecks of the Western Hemisphere*, there are recorded ancient wrecks in the waters around St Vincent. He mentions that, in 1635, two Spanish merchant ships were wrecked on the south eastern tip of the island and that survivors were found some 32 years later, in 1667, by English settlers arriving on St Vincent. However, known and diveable wreck sites which are available are more modern, three of them being situated in Kingstown harbour.

On 21 November 1984, the 120 ft freighter **Seimstrand** collided with another freighter, the **Nomad**, and both sank next to each other.

The top deck of the *Nomad* is in only 15 ft of water, gradually sloping to 40 ft. Just behind, the *Seimstrand* starts in 60 ft sloping down to 80 ft. A pair of large French angelfish make the wrecks their permanent home and can be seen on every dive. Small trees of black coral, yellow and orange sponges adorn the decks. Numerous locations offer ideal photographic opportunities.

A little deeper, at 100 ft, an exposed cannon, a large anchor and several bathtubs can be seen. It is thought that they may belong to the HMS *Cornwall* or to the slave ship *Africa*, according to the limited research done on this subject. However, the ship which contributed these items remains a mystery. Near the wrecks, a patch of coral formations is home for numerous fish and in particular the colourful frog fish.

To the south, the islands of the Grenadines which belong to St Vincent – Union Island, Canouan, Mayreau, Mustique and Bequia – offer too some interesting diving.

At Bequia, an easy beginners' dive is **Devils Table**, a 45 ft reef in calm water, only 5 minutes by boat from the dive shops . It is also an excellent site for a night dive. Underwater channels on a sandy bottom wind through the coral formation. Azure vase sponges adorn the wall, along with the more common types of sponges. Puffer fish and frog fish, not a common sight, and large green moray can be spotted.

The Wall, on West Cay, is a very dramatic, sheer wall. Its depth and the occasional presence of currents restrict it to experienced divers. It starts at 12 ft, dropping to 30 ft where it forms a ledge. From 30 ft, a sheer drop begins as one descends to reach a sandy bottom at 120 ft. Occasionally a black tip shark will swim by or one may sight a nurse shark resting under an overhang. Black coral and sea fans adorn the face of the drop off. Moray eels and lobsters are found tucked into nooks and crannies, along with small invertebrate life such as coral banded shrimp and large anemones.

The **Boulders** is a drift dive. Drifting in an average depth of 60 ft, divers view large coral covered boulders on a sandy bottom. Encrusted rock formations create tunnels and passages. The currents and the need to manoeuvre among the boulders make this site unsuitable for a novice diver, although one of the shops describes it as 'suitable for the experienced beginner' . . . Marine life is diverse; small gentle sea horses, plume worms, flamingo tongues feeding on sea fans and feather dusters drifting back and forth in the current are part of the beautiful scenery. Larger life

such as barracuda and the occasional shark give a touch of excitement.

The **Gladdie**, a 65 ft wreck, lies in 90 ft of water, port side down. She was a cement sailboat which, in her sailing days, plied the waters around the islands. The *Gladdie* is intact and divers can swim through the superstructure. She was deliberately sunk in 1978 by the Bequia authorities as a diving site. Spade fish, large angelfish and green moray eels are a common sight with the occasional nurse shark. The depth makes it suitable for advanced divers only.

Union, Canouan, Mayreau and Mustique have also their special sites.

One of the favourites, in this area, is the 140 ft World War I English gunboat HMS **Purina**, which lies just off Mayreau in only 40 ft of water, with the top deck in a mere 23 ft, making it an ideal beginners' dive. In 1918, during a normal patrol, when the British were protecting the area, the HMS *Purina* hit the reef and immediately sank, sitting upright in the shallow water. She is totally intact, with boilers, several heads and two massive propellers still in place. Due to the shallow depth, she is encrusted with luxuriant growth of hard and soft corals and inhabited by lobsters and octopus, along with a varied invertebrate life.

Mayreau Gardens, part of the Tobago Keys National Park and a protected site, is located between Mayreau and the Tobago Keys. This is a drift dive, beginning in 40 ft of water, and depending on the current, divers can either drift in a northerly or southerly direction, with the reef to the south dropping to 85 ft while the northern one remains around 60 ft. The boat drifts over the divers rather than anchoring. Divers will come across barracuda and nurse sharks as well as sting rays resting on the sandy bottom, in between coral formations. As the coral slopes down, overhangs and ledges are home for a wide array of marine life.

Diver with grey angelfish

Horseshoe Reef, an 80 ft dive, also in the protected area, offers beautiful coral formations and its own resident huge jew fish, who hides under a deep overhang. Soft gorgonia and a wide assortment of hard corals make up the reef structure.

For the very experienced diver, **Sail Rocks** is an exciting site which can only be reached in very calm seas. This rock outcropping, located to the east of the islands, is in open ocean and provides a collection of marine life. It is a drift dive as divers enter the water on the windward side allowing the strong currents to sweep them completely round the rocks. As many as 100 barracuda and several dozen nurse sharks can be spotted at one time. Turtles often swim by, along with pelagic life. Because of the currents and the presence of large life, only advanced divers are taken to Sail Rocks.

St Vincent and the Grenadines are a pristine dive destination which deserves to be explored, especially given the organization that has developed between the various dive shops, enabling divers to discover a large number of sites at reasonable rates.

Directory

St Vincent

Dive St Vincent
(Owner) Bill Tewes
Box 864
St Vincent, West Indies
TELEPHONE 809 457 4928/4714
FAX 809 457 4948

Bequia

Dive Bequia
(Owner) Bob Sachs
Box 16
Bequia, St Vincent, West Indies
TELEPHONE 809 458 3425   FAX 809 458 3886

Union

Grenadines Dive
(Owner) Glenroy Adams
Sunny Grenadines Hotel
Union Island, St Vincent, West Indies
(Business) TELEPHONE 809 458 8138
(Home) TELEPHONE AND FAX 809 458 8122

Canouan

Dive Canouan
(Owner) John Monaghan
Canouan Beach Hotel
Canouan, St Vincent, West Indies
TELEPHONE 809 458 8648   FAX 809 458 8875

• For further information, contact:

St Vincent and Grenadines Tourist Board
located on Egmont Street
Box 834
Kingstown, St Vincent, West Indies
TELEPHONE 809 457 1502   FAX 809 457 1502

USA:
801 Second Ave, 21st Floor
New York, New York 10017
TELEPHONE 212 949 5946   FAX 800 729 1726

UK:
c/o Organization of Eastern Caribbean States
Suite 437
High Holborn House
52 High Holborn
London WC1V 6RB
TELEPHONE 071 242 3131